Lake Ilmen, 1942

To our friend and master historian, Carlos Caballero Jurado

Lake Ilmen, 1942

The Wehrmacht Front to the Red Army

PABLO SAGARRA AND ÓSCAR GONZÁLEZ
TRANSLATED BY STEVE TURPIN WHITE

Pen & Sword
MILITARY
AN IMPRINT OF PEN & SWORD BOOKS LTD.
YORKSHIRE - PHILADELPHIA

First published in 2016 by Galland Books as *Lago Ilmen, 1942*

First published in Great Britain in 2019 by
Pen & Sword Military
An imprint of
Pen & Sword Books Ltd
Yorkshire - Philadelphia

ISBN 978 1 52671 993 5

Typeset by Aura Technology and Software Services, India
Printed and bound in India
by Replika Press Pvt. Ltd.

Pen & Sword Books Ltd incorporates the Imprints of Pen & Sword Books Archaeology, Atlas, Aviation, Battleground, Discovery, Family History, History, Maritime, Military, Naval, Politics, Railways, Select, Transport, True Crime, Fiction, Frontline Books, Leo Cooper, Praetorian Press, Seaforth Publishing, Wharncliffe and White Owl.

For a complete list of Pen & Sword titles please contact

PEN & SWORD BOOKS LIMITED
47 Church Street, Barnsley, South Yorkshire, S70 2AS, England
E-mail: enquiries@pen-and-sword.co.uk
Website: www.pen-and-sword.co.uk

or

PEN AND SWORD BOOKS
1950 Lawrence Rd, Havertown, PA 19083, USA
E-mail: uspen-and-sword@casematepublishers.com
Website: www.penandswordbooks.com

Contents

Acknowledgements   7

Introduction   8

1 Strategic Framework: The "Winter" Generals, Zhukov,
   Kurochkin and Morozov, Take the Initiative   11

2 Encirclement of the German Garrisons of Vzvad
   and Staraya Russa   26

3 Creation and Deployment of the 250th Ski Company
   of the Blue Division   46

4 The Lake Crossing by the Spanish Troops   71

5 Containment Engagements to the South of Lake Ilmen
   and Evacuation of Vzvad   85

6 Conclusions Regarding Fighting Spirit, Tactics and Strategy   109

7 Remembrance and Significance   117

Appendix   122

Sources   128

Acknowledgements

We would like to thank all Blue Division members (hereinafter *divisionarios*) and the families of *divisionarios* mentioned in the sources for having told us their stories and given us access to their private archives. We are also grateful to all the owners or custodians of the photographic archives which have helped illustrate this book, and to other sources of help, including Gonzalo and Daniel, administrators of the *Memoriablau* Internet forum, Jaime Barriuso, Antonio Bermejo Aybar, Carlos Caballero Jurado, Elsa de Miguel Grigans, Jesús Dolado, Jesús Gómez Gómez-Jareño, Ángel G. Pinilla, Boris Kovalev, Manuel Liñán, José María Manrique, Lucas Molina Franco, Juan Negreira, Peregrín Pascual, *Second Lieutenant* Pastor, Manuel Pérez Rubio, Antonio Prieto Barrio, José Manuel Puente, Jaime Sadurní, José Antonio Saez López, Germán Segura, Francisco Torres, and Blas Vicente Marco.

Translator's Note
Given that soldiers of three nationalities were involved in the Lake Ilmen story, for the sake of readability it was decided, as a general rule, to translate the names of ranks and medals into English.

Introduction

"Man can only come to know himself by doing"

(Goethe)

In January 1942, in the Staraya Russa sector to the south of Lake Ilmen, Soviet and German forces engaged in a fierce and protracted battle. A tiny number of Spaniards, the Ski Company of the 250th Division of the *Wehrmacht*, the Spanish Blue Division, was involved in that battle for a little over twenty days.

In the context of the Russian Front at that time, immersed in the general offensive launched by the Red Army in that first winter of the war in Russia, this episode was of no great importance. It was one of the countless events of the clash between two gigantic forces, the German and Soviet armies which, let us not forget, was to determine the military outcome of the Second World War.

The action known by the Spanish as the *"Gesta del Lago Ilmen"* (Heroic feat at Lake Ilmen) was not an isolated action of the Blue Division. Rather it was one which, along with other feats of arms in the campaign against Communism, and regardless of the part played by luck, a factor which unquestionably influenced the outcome of the operation, formed part of a strategic project of far-reaching importance: the German defence of Staraya Russa.

With this work we aim to shine a light on Spanish involvement in the first winter battle south of Lake Ilmen. We focus not so much on its undeniable qualities as a feat of arms, already well documented by Spanish and non-Spanish historians, both past and contemporary, but rather on its human aspect - by studying those who took part - and its tactical and strategic importance.

The historiographical approach that we have been pursuing for some years now, with the aid of primary sources of a personal and private nature (testimonies, diaries, correspondence, etc.), will enable us to gain a more in-depth knowledge and understanding of a number of the volunteers who left sunny Spain to fight in northern Russia. We will also be focusing on several highly skilled commanders, almost as young as the men they led, also volunteers and with combat experience in the 1936-1939 Civil War.

1. Badge of the Collective Military Medal awarded to participants in the Lake Ilmen action. (Ramiro Bujeiro)

2. Plaque or panel in remembrance of the operations at Lake Ilmen, probably made by one of the units of the 16th Army. Unofficial commemorative elements of this kind were made by the same German Army units involved in the actions. Miniature versions were often handed out to soldiers and used on the cover of books published by the unit. Larger versions were used in the gardens or on buildings of the barracks back in Germany. (Authors' collection)

3. German infantry operating in woodland during the first winter of the campaign. (Authors' collection)

We also aim to expand on and complement the narrative of other Spanish, German and Russian authors. Some concern themselves more with recounting the action as a typically Spanish feat; others pay the action little heed, seeing it as an insignificant event in the terrible series of engagements that took place during that winter in almost every sector of Army Group North, particularly the German pockets at Cholm and Demyansk and the Soviet pocket of the Volkhov. Russian historians' lack of interest in this action is especially understandable, as it was just another episode in the doomed Staraya Russa offensive, a large-scale operation that is largely ignored by Russian historians, who prefer to recount other more successful counter-offensives.

Strategic Framework: The "Winter" Generals, Zhukov, Kurochkin and Morozov, Take the Initiative

On 2 December 1941, the Motorcycle Battalion of the *Deutschland* Regiment of the 2nd *Panzerdivision* SS *Das Reich* pushed through the suburbs surrounding Moscow reaching as far as the end of the city's trolleybus line, just 22 km from the Red Square and the Kremlin. The advance units of Guderian's II *Panzer* Group were at Kashira, some 120 km to the south, while the *Luftwaffe* punished the capital of Stalin's empire from the air in preparation for an attack which never came.

Around this same date, much further to the north-west, several battalions and support units of the 250th Infantry Division, the Spanish Blue Division attached to *General* Ernst Busch's 16th Army, were fighting at the bridgehead to the east of the River Volkhov. They had been locked in battle for several weeks with the men of Klykov's 52nd Russian Army in an attempt to support the planned advance of the German 126th Division towards Borovichi on their southern flank (from where

German troops in the Staraya Russa zone in August 1941. (AHSR)

The winter of 1941-1942 in northern Russia surprised the *Wehrmacht*, stretching it to the limit of its logistical capabilities. (Authors' collection)

they aimed to link up with the forces of Army Group Centre at Kalinin). These actions were carried out in combination with the general attack of the XXXIX Army Corps which, on 9 November, had succeeded in occupying Tikhvin, 470 km to the east of Leningrad. This axis of attack was later intended to reach the River Svir and so make it impossible to supply Leningrad via Lake Ladoga.

At this stage of *Barbarossa* (the code name given to the Axis invasion of the USSR and the destruction of its army), German troops had reached the furthest point of the gigantic advance they had embarked upon on 22 June. Six months later, the logistical rubber band, stretched to its limit from the Russo-Polish border, was at breaking point and threatened to cause a breakdown of "Napoleonic proportions" (similar to the one suffered by Napoleon's *Grande Armée* in the winter of 1812).

Faced with the evidence that Army Group Centre's offensive had fizzled out, on the night of 5 December *General* Von Bock ordered a halt to the offensive on Moscow. His armoured divisions were to withdraw in order to avoid being engulfed by fresh Soviet units which were to initiate a counter-offensive the following day. In Von Leeb's Army Group North things were no better, the XXXIX Army Corps being forced to leave Tikhvin on 9 December. In the early hours of the previous day, in anticipation of orders from German command, the 250th Spanish Division had returned to the positions they had held the previous October, on the west bank of the River Volkhov.

Withdrawing in defiance of Hitler's wishes, the *Wehrmacht* suffered but remained intact. The forces of nature, insufficient military forces, and the renewed Soviet push prompted a German withdrawal which, despite the circumstances, was relatively orderly. The counter-offensive to save Moscow conducted throughout December, led by *General* (later *Marshal*) Zhukov and supported by an unusually cold *General* "Winter", had forced Army Group Centre to fall back towards the west by a distance of between 150-400 km (depending on the sector), almost as

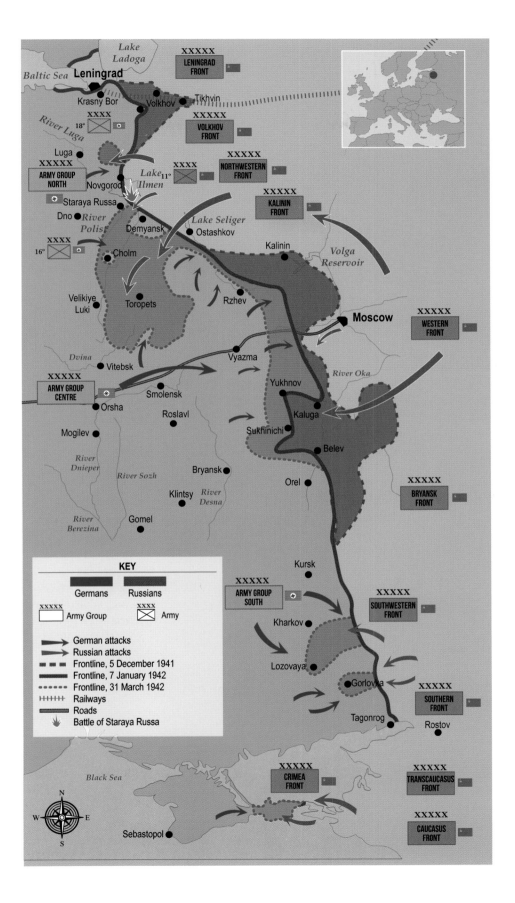

KEY

Germans Russians

XXXXX Army Group XXXX Army

→ German attacks
→ Russian attacks
- - - Frontline, 5 December 1941
——— Frontline, 7 January 1942
· · · · Frontline, 31 March 1942
+++++ Railways
——— Roads
↘ Battle of Staraya Russa

Lake Ladoga
Baltic Sea
Leningrad
Krasny Bor
Volkhov
Tikhvin
XXXXX LENINGRAD FRONT
River Luga
XXXX 18°
XXXXX VOLKHOV FRONT
Luga
XXXXX ARMY GROUP NORTH
Novgorod
Lake Ilmen 11°
XXXX 11°
XXXXX NORTHWESTERN FRONT
Staraya Russa
Dno
River Polist
Demyansk
Lake Seliger
Ostashkov
XXXXX KALININ FRONT
XXXX 16°
Cholm
Kalinin
Volga Reservoir
Velikiye Luki
Toropets
Rzhev
Dvina
Vitebsk
Vyazma
Moscow
XXXXX WESTERN FRONT
XXXXX ARMY GROUP CENTRE
Orsha
Smolensk
Roslavl
Yukhnov
Kaluga
River Oka
Sukhinichi
Belev
River Dnieper
River Sozh
Bryansk
Orel
XXXXX BRYANSK FRONT
Mogilev
Klintsy
River Desna
River Berezina
Gomel
Kursk
XXXXX ARMY GROUP SOUTH
XXXXX SOUTHWESTERN FRONT
Kharkov
Lozovaya
Gorlovka
XXXXX SOUTHERN FRONT
Tagonrog
Rostov
Black Sea
XXXXX CRIMEA FRONT
XXXXX TRANSCAUCASUS FRONT
Sebastopol
XXXXX CAUCASUS FRONT

N
W E
S

far as the Smolensk line from where Operation "Typhoon" had begun the previous 15 October. As already mentioned, the troops of the neighbouring Army Group North of Von Leeb had also been forced to fall back, while fighting off increasingly heavy enemy attacks.

On the freezing Russian Front from Lake Ladoga to the Black Sea, New Year 1942 was celebrated in thousands of shelters and command posts with mixed feelings. For the Reich and its allies the attempt to capture Moscow was a distant memory; the festivities were bittersweet as the troops were all aware that the Communists were a very hard nut to crack. Now, having been given the order to resist by Hitler from his *Wolfsschanze* (Wolf's Lair) in East Prussia, their task was to withstand the enemy counter-offensive that they knew would be coming. Meanwhile, despite the crippling losses in men and materiel suffered in previous months and despite the precarious nature of the supplies reaching frontline soldiers, for the Russians hope and optimism were the predominant sentiments, because they fully expected to deal a merciless blow to the invaders.

The defensive line of Army Group North was ready for battle. Pivoting on lakes Ladoga, Ilmen and Seliger (at the latter lake joining up with Army Group Centre), nearly thirty divisions belonging to the 18th and 16th Armies were waiting to be attacked by two Soviet army groups: the Volkhov Front commanded by *General* Kirill Meretskov and the North-West Front led by *General* Kurochkin.

1. A dispatch rider of the Division *Das Reich* views the domes of the New Jerusalem Monastery of Resurrection at Istra, 50 km from Moscow. (HIAG – Mutual aid association of former Waffen-SS members)

2. Scenes like this column of Soviet prisoners of war in the region of Pskov in the summer 1941 were unimaginable just six months later. (AHSR)

ZHUKOV
Soviet General

Georgy Konstantinovich Zhukov, possibly the most brilliant Russian commander in the Second World War, was born in 1898. He came to the fore in 1939 when fighting the Japanese, employing the mobile war tactics already championed by the late General Tukhachevsky. Zhukov played a major role in the battles of Moscow, Leningrad, Stalingrad, and Kursk, as well as in Operation Bagration and the capture of Berlin. After the war, due to his popularity in the Soviet Army and the good relationship he had with Eisenhower, Stalin removed him from the command of any major unit and stationed him away from Moscow. After Stalin's death he became Minister of Defence. He retired in 1960 and died of a heart attack in 1974.

The apparent calm was broken between 4-8 January 1942, when the grand Soviet general offensive was set in motion, the main objective of which was the German strategic centre of gravity, that is to say, Army Group Centre's enormous salient. In this clash between two colossal armies, the Blue Division was naturally in the firing line.

3. Zhukov was the architect of the defence of Moscow. (Authors' collection)

4. Spanish shelters in the first winter. (Ordás family collection)

ОТСТОИМ МОСКВУ!

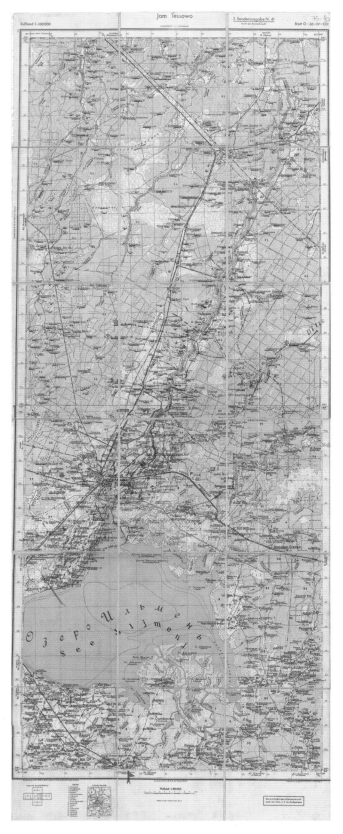

However, as luck would have it, and because the Soviet commanders had already discovered how hard they were to break, the Spanish troops escaped the brunt of the Russian onslaught. This is apparent from the regular bulletins of the 2nd Staff Platoon Information of the Blue Division which provide information regarding the campaign, the organization and disposition of the enemy, its intentions, mood and morale, etc. Bulletin no. 29 of 2 January 1942 stated that: *"it is confirmed that the enemy's morale is very low. This low morale is more accentuated among the units that have fought against our Division."* Bulletin no. 36, dated 17 January 1942, said: *"All statements made by deserters suggest a marked drop in the enemy's morale compared to that of our Division. The political commissars have spoken to them these days and have told them that the manoeuvre that is under way is aimed at overrunning our Division from the north so as to avoid a frontal attack, which the enemy commander is keen to avoid due to the number of casualties they suffer whenever they attack our Division. According to these same prisoners, the Russian soldiers say that their 30th Division has been almost wiped out by our Spanish Division and that they prefer fighting against German units."* For whatever reason, a relative calm reigned over the Spanish sector while neighbouring divisions were heavily attacked and penetrated.

Location of the Ski Company on the Blue Division Front in December 1941. (Authors' collection)

KUROCHKIN
Commander of the Soviet North-West Front (January 1942)

Pavel Alekseyevich Kurochkin was born on 28 November 1900. He joined the Bolshevik Party and the Red Army, becoming a member of the All-Russian Communist Party in 1918. In the Russian Civil War he commanded cavalry units. In the Second World War, after commanding a number of large units in the containment battles against the German invaders, he was sent to the North-West Front (of which Morozov's 11th Army formed part), which was responsible for attacking the German 16th Army to the south of Lake Ilmen in January 1942. He ended the war as Commander-in-Chief of the 60th Army. In his post-war career he held a number of very senior positions, including chairman of the Supreme Command of the United Military Forces of the Warsaw Pact. A Hero of the Soviet Union, he died in Moscow, in 1989, just before the break-up of the State to which he had dedicated his life.

From the Blue Division's point of view, the most serious of the Russian penetrations, due to it being the closest and the most dangerous, affected its northern flank where the Soviet Volkhov Front (the 52nd Army and the 2nd Shock Army) succeeded in opening up a breach between the German 126th and 215th Divisions. This breach, with the passage of time, would end up becoming an enormous Russian pocket which would survive, active and defiant, until well into the following summer. Several Spanish units would play an active role in containing and then annihilating the Volkhov Pocket in the following six months.

The attack from south of Lake Ilmen was potentially as lethal as the attack from the north. As we have said, the Russians wanted to take advantage of the exposed situation of the entire German sector between Lake Ilmen and Lake Seliger. At the southernmost end of this latter lake was where the North and Centre Army Groups converged. The *Stavka*'s ambitious plan was to pierce the German line at the point where those two Army Groups met. In this way they would, on the one hand, destroy the rearguard of Army Group Centre, penetrating beyond Smolensk, and on the other, in the sector which concerns us, after taking Staraya Russa, they would advance along the west bank of the Ilmen, turn towards Luga, and so link up with Volkhov Front forces and roll up the remaining units of the 16th Army, among others, the Blue Division.

According to the Soviet plan, the 11th Army of *General* Vasiliy Ivanovich Morozov would launch the offensive along the southern bank of the Ilmen in line with the 34th Army of *General* Nikolai Berzarin. Initially, Vasily Ivanovich

DEPLOYMENT 16th ARMY (1 JANUARY 1942)

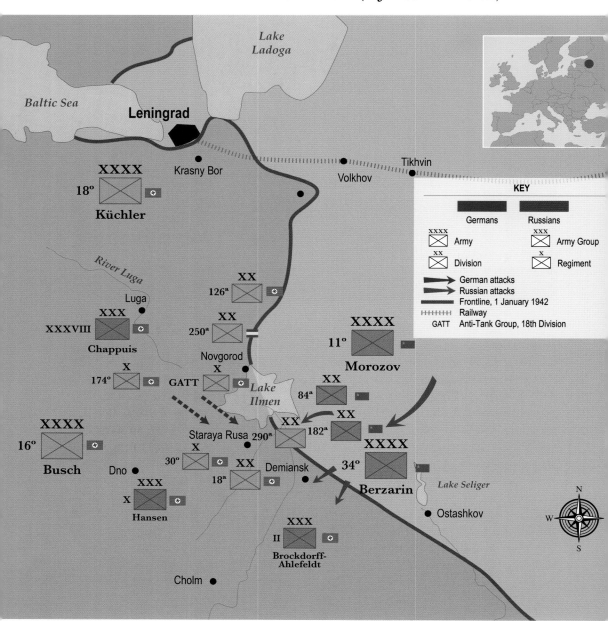

Kuznetsov's 1st Shock Army was also assigned to the attack on Staraya Russa, but it would be withdrawn from the line as a *Stavka* reserve to be used to seal off and crush the Demyansk Pocket. Three armies would advance over Lake Seliger and from the Valdai Heights: the 3rd and 4th Shock Armies and the 22nd Army.

Dno, an important communications hub of the 16th Army. (Authors' collection)

Crossroads to the west of Lake Ilmen signposting the most important towns of the sector in which the fighting in January 1942 took place. (FDA)

GENERAL INVIERNO

Lake Ilmen

Lake Ilmen is the most important geo-strategic reference in the region. It is roughly triangular in shape, with an extension of a little over 2,000 km², and measures 45 km east-west and 38 km north-south at its widest points. Surrounded by dense forest and extensive marshland, it is fed by four major rivers, the Msta, the Pola, the Lovat, and the Shelon. Its waters flow northwards, through the River Volkhov which discharges into Lake Ladoga. On its banks, just as there were so many decades ago, there are still a number of fishing villages, some of them with services catering for tourists.

Given the immensity of the lake, in the summer of 1941 when the *Wehrmacht* reached its banks, the lines of the two opposing forces were very far apart.

The Germans occupied the west and southern banks of the lake while the Russians were on the eastern shore. The lake was of no importance until the winter cold turned its water into ice. It then became a terrain which, while not fit for fighting on, did present a possible route for infantry and armoured forces to advance over, given that the half metre thick ice could bear the weight of vehicles as heavy as tanks. Once frozen, Lake Ilmen acquired a far greater strategic importance than it had had a few weeks earlier.

The surface of the lake was irregular due to the pressure of the currents trapped by the ice, which in the middle of the lake, aided by the snow and the wind, had formed impassable crevasses, icebergs and barriers. The temperature in the heart of that icy wasteland was below -50 °C. From the surface of the lake rose a searing icy mist that made any movement of men and animals an onerous task. This white, referencelesss landscape was where the Spanish skiers had to operate.

"Lake Ilmen, Lake Ilmen,
What a story you have to tell.
On you there are traces of blood,
On you there is Spanish bravery.
On you heroes revelled
Under that majestic night,
And they felt more like martyrs
Because the blood was purer.
They looked like white ghosts
On a night of witches,
They groaned with weariness,
With pain, with anguish,
Yet continued marching
Giving no encouragement to doubt.
Ay, my mother, my mother!
Ay, my bride of whiteness!
I am sweating sorrows
And you are crying like never before.
I am forging my destiny
And you will embroider
A shawl that the Blessed Virgin
Will fill with beauty.
My God, what a cruel ordeal!
What a night like no other
What a holy caravan
Under the canopy of the moon.
Farewell, farewell Lake Ilmen,
What a story you have to tell."

Alberto del Pozo. Infantry soldier. *Hoja de Campaña*. Russia 2-IX-1942

Staraya Russa

Staraya Russa (in Russian *Старая Русса* and in German *Staraja Russa*), captured early on in Operation *Barbarossa*, became the logistics centre of the German sector between Lake Ilmen and Lake Seliger. Being a key communications hub, a significant amount of supplies and services of the Army Corps II and X of the 16th Army were amassed there.

Holding Staraya Russa was vital because it dominated a region of marshland and forest and also because it was traversed by a high capacity railway line, running between Dno, around which the entire rearguard of the German Army Group North was based, and the Soviet-held town of Valday on the main road between Moscow and Leningrad.

Against this formidable mass of manoeuvre, consisting partly of fresh troops, the units of Busch's 16th Army which formed the right flank of Army Group North, and which would therefore bear the brunt of the initial attack, were not in the best of shape, having been fighting without a break for months. They could field six infantry divisions: three of the X Army Corps under the command of *General* Hansen (290th, 30th and the 3rd SS *Totenkopf*) and another three belonging to *General* Brockdorff-Ahlefeldt's II Army Corps (123rd, 32nd and 12th). Later other units were to become involved; these will be mentioned as they appear.

Let us now take a look at the events that were to unfold during the weeks to come on the southern flank of the 16th Army, since this was where the Spanish Ski Company would carry out their remarkable exploit.

During the night of 7-8 January 1942, without any previous artillery preparation, Kurochkin's North-West Front began to advance. Battalions of the 11th Army, supported by tanks, moved forward over the ice and through the forests to the south of Lake Ilmen, breaking the line held by the 290th Division. On the third day, while the German positions were destroyed or their defenders were pushed back (save for those at Vzvad, who were encircled), Morozov ran into difficulties near Staraya Russa. However, further to the south in the Lake Seliger sector, Kurochkin was having much more success. His 3rd and 4th Shock Armies (these would be later be transferred to the Kalinin Front), with their flank protected by the 22nd Army, overwhelmed the 123rd Division in a rapid advance.

Wintery landscape in the Blue Division sector. (Juan Negreira)

The front defended by the German 16th Army to the south of the Ilmen had been penetrated in so many places it began to resemble a Swiss cheese. Many of its major units were either forced to withdraw or were encircled. Busch was in desperate need of reinforcements.

Von Leeb realized the seriousness of the situation; his 16th Army was in mortal danger and he was considering falling back to the River Lovat. Hitler, however, preferred to replace him on 17 January with *Generalfeldmarschall* von Küchler – hitherto commander of the 18th Army –, who was ordered to hold on at all cost.

Two large Soviet pincers began to form, while all German positions were defended tooth and nail. Just a few weeks later, on 8 February, the 11th and 1st Shock Armies linked up, sealing the encirclement of the battered German divisions and giving rise to the huge Demyansk Pocket and, further to the south-west, to the much smaller Cholm Pocket. But by then the intervention of the Ski Company to the south of Lake Ilmen had finished and the survivors were already back with the Blue Division.

1. German lines of communications were tested to breaking point by the polar cold. (Authors' collection)

2. Horse-drawn sled with Spanish soldiers in the Lake Ilmen sector in the winter of 1941-1942. (Authors' collection)

Army Group North

GENERALFELDMARSCHALL
Wilhelm Ritter von Leeb

GENERALFELDMARSCHALL
Georg von Küchler
(as from 17 January 1942)

16th Army

GENERALFELDMARSCHALL
Ernst Bernhard Wilhelm Busch

18th Army

GENERALFELDMARSCHALL
Georg von Küchler

GENERAL
Georg Heinrich Lindemann
(as from 17 January 1942)

16th Army

XXXVIII ARMY CORPS
GENERAL Friedrich Wilhelm
von Chappuis

X ARMY CORPS
GENERAL Christian Hansen

II ARMY CORPS
GENERAL Walter von
Brockdorff-Ahlefeldt

126th INFANTRY DIVISION
GENERAL Paul Laux

290th INFANTRY DIVISION
GENERAL Theodor Freiherr
von Wrede

123rd INFANTRY DIVISION
GENERAL Erwin Rauch

250th INFANTRY DIVISION
GENERAL Agustín Muñoz
Grandes

30th INFANTRY DIVISION
GENERAL Kurt von
Tippelskirch

32nd INFANTRY DIVISION
GENERAL Wilhelm
Bohnstedt

81st INFANTRY DIVISION
GENERAL Erich Hermann
Schopper (until 9 January 1942)

18th INFANTRY DIVISION
GENERAL Werner von
Erdmannsdorff

12th INFANTRY DIVISION
OBERST Karl Hernekamp

COMBAT GROUP
81st INFANTRY DIVISION,
FROM 10 JANUARY 1942.

3rd WAFFEN-SS
***TOTENKOPF* DIVISION**
GENERAL Theodor Eicke
(until 22 January 1942)

3rd WAFFEN-SS
***TOTENKOPF* DIVISION**
GENERAL Theodor Eicke
(from 22 January 1942)

Encirclement of the German Garrisons of Vzvad and Staraya Russa

Now we have seen the strategic context, let us move to Vzvad, a fishing village of 200 *izbas* (or typical rural houses), located in the marshland where the River Lovat feeds into the south side of Lake Ilmen.

It had been occupied by the *Wehrmacht* early in September 1941, albeit very lightly. But once the lake had frozen over, turning it into a "no man's ice" as the Spanish called it - in other words a terrain that could be crossed by infiltrating enemy troops - the German commanders, led by one *Captain* Günther Pröhl, had reinforced their garrison.

From the five divisions of Morozov's 11ᵗʰ Army, the 84ᵗʰ and 182ⁿᵈ Rifle Divisions were chosen to attack across Lake Ilmen and around its southern shores. As the rest of the defences of the 290ᵗʰ Infantry Division collapsed, the German forward line at Vzvad, 16 km to the north-east of Staraya Russa, became of enormous importance to the sector, despite the fact that it was defended by a little over

A preserved T-26 in Novgorod. (Authors' collection)

500 men. The existence of a *Luftwaffe* "Freya" radar in the town made it all the more important and was one more factor behind its initial heroic defence.

At 20.35 on 8 January 1942, well into the hours of darkness, fighting broke out between the 140th Regiment and the Vzvad garrison. Both sides suffered casualties, especially the Russians, who also had a number of prisoners taken by the Germans. *Captain* Pröhl tried to link up with *Lieutenant-Colonel* Iffland, the commander of his unit, by radio but was unable to make contact. So instead he contacted the commander of the X Army Corps, *General* Hansen, informing of events and passing on what he had gleaned from Russian prisoners who said there was to be a large scale offensive on Staraya Russa.

Ribbon of the Commemorative Medal for Spanish Volunteers in the Fight against Bolshevism, instituted by Hitler on 3 January 1944 for members of the Blue Division and Blue Squadrons. (Authors' collection)

A sled in the 16th German Army sector. (Authors' collection)

GÜNTHER PRÖHL

Günther Pröhl was born on 14 March 1895 in the city of Schwerin, the capital of Mecklenburg-West Pomerania. After taking part in the First World War, during the Weimar Republic years he embraced National Socialist ideology. He joined the National Socialist Automobile Corps (NSAK), founded in April 1930, the predecessor of the NSKK *(Nationalsozialistisches Kraftfahrkorps)*, a paramilitary organization of the Nazi Party dedicated to instructing and training its members in all things automotive.

Pröhl worked for the NSKK in Kiel, a coastal city in Germany. After Hitler came to power, Pröhl gradually climbed the ranks of the organization; by 9 November 1935 he was a *Brigadeführer*, a rank slightly higher than *Oberst* (Colonel) in the army, and two years later, on 6 September 1937, he was promoted to *Gruppenführer*, equivalent to *Generalleutnant* (Lieutenant General) in the German Army.

In Operation *Barbarossa*, Günther Pröhl fought as commander of the Anti-Tank Group *(Jagdpanzer)* of the 290th Infantry Division, deployed to the south of Lake Ilmen. In January 1942, as commander of the Vzvad garrison, he withstood a thirteen day long siege by outnumbering Soviet forces. He finally abandoned the position, with authorization from above, and made it back to his own lines with the bulk of his men. His determined resistance at Vzvad was greatly exploited in German propaganda and he was rewarded with a coveted Knight's Cross and promotion in the ranks of the NSKK to *Obergruppenführer* (equivalent to *General* in the German Army).

Shortly afterwards he would be appointed commander of *Abteilung I* of the NSKK in the civil administration of the *Reichskommissariat Ostland* (the *Reich* Commissariat for the eastern occupied territories), the organization responsible for the Germanization and ethnic cleansing of the Baltic territories, and for settling ethnic Germans in the occupied areas. After the commissariat was dissolved because of the way the war was going, he was transferred to Hamburg, where he commanded the *Volkssturm*, the city's people's militia. Günther Pröhl survived the war (by the end of which he had risen to the rank of major in the German Army, after promotion in 1943) and died in Ahrensburg, a town to the north-east of Hamburg, on 19 November 1977.

Hansen ordered Pröhl to resist and hold his position, assuring him that the *Luftwaffe* would be dropping provisions, and reported what was happening to the south of Lake Ilmen to his superior officer, *General* Busch. Thus a new fighting front was opened up for the 16th Army, to add to the one opened up four days previously in the 126th Division's sector. Busch reported to *General* Von Leeb, commander-in-Chief of Army Group North, who was concerned to see the growing pressure exerted by the Red Army, from the Volkhov to Lake Ladoga. He therefore had to be very cautious when sending in reserves. Inexorably, the commander's attention was drawn towards the 81st Silesian Infantry Division, which was about to reach the zone of operations.

Spanish soldiers with skis; a Russian child stands in the foreground. (Senent family collection)

VZVAD GARRISON

In accordance with orders from the 16th Army, the Vzvad garrison (Wswad in German) was under the command of the highest ranking officer present, in this case *Captain* Günther Pröhl, head of the Anti-Tank Group (*Jagdpanzer*) of the 290th Division (*Panzerjäger Abteilung 290*).

Pröhl had 543 men belonging to various units: his own *Jagdpanzer* Group, the 38th Motorcycle Battalion (*Kradschützen Bataillon 38*) of the 18th Motorized Division, the 2nd Company of the 615th Guard Battalion (*Wachbataillon 615*), the 6th Company of the 1st Signals Regiment of the *Luftwaffe* (6./*Luftwaffe Nachrichten Regiment* 1), and the local Russian collaborator militia, led by Viktor Nikolayevich, known among his fellow countrymen as "The Counsellor".

Of this hotchpotch of troops the most capable fighters were to be found among the *Jagdpanzer* Group, among the Motorcycle Battalion troops who had taken refuge in Pröhl's position, and among the 80 volunteers of the Russian anti-communist militia, since the Guard Battalion was formed by elderly men and the *Luftwaffe* company was not really a combat unit.

Against this background we need to bear in mind the intentions of *General* Von Chappuis, commander of the XXXVIII Army Corps, regarding the Blue Division. This old-school Prussian officer had little faith in the Division, despite the resilience that it had displayed in the campaign so far, and he had asked Busch to replace it with German forces. If he could not remove the Division from the front, Chappuis, whose command post was in Raglizy, to the north-west of Novgorod, wanted at least to have

them moved further south and shorten its line of contact with the enemy along the shore of Lake Ilmen between Novgorod and Staraya Russa. He went as far as to propose building a line of wooden blockhouses along the west bank and locating Muñoz Grandes' headquarters at Shimsk, at the far south-west end of the lake.

According to the original plan, and in response to Chappuis' oppressive insistence, the bulk of the 81st Division had started to deploy in Novgorod. In fact, on 5 January 1942, its commander-in-chief, *General* Erich Hermann Schopper, had been appointed commander of the rearguard of the XXXVIII Army Corps, and his 174th Regiment, billeted a few kilometres away from Novgorod, was ready to relieve the Blue Division. News of their possible relief had reached the ears of the Spanish Division, as is reflected, for example, in the diary of José Guillén Marquina, serving with the Medical Group, who as late as 9 January wrote: *"Guard duty gossip: that the relief of the 250th Division by the 81st is already a fact, and the Germans are complaining about how slowly it is being carried out."*

However, on 10 January Schopper was excused from his duties in the rearguard of the XXXVIII Army Corps and, at the head of a strong combat group formed by units of his Division, hurried off in the direction of the Staraya Russa sector.

1. German troops watching women dancing in the Staraya Russa sector to the south of Lake Ilmen. (AHSR)

2. A driver of a KV-1, the much feared Soviet tank which was present at the Battle of Staraya Russa. (Za Rodinu)

THE "FREYA" RADAR AT VZVAD

At the "Vzvad Support Point" (*Stützpunkt*) the *Luftwaffe* had a core of air observers (*Flugmelde Funk Kompanie*) belonging to the 1st Air District Signals Regiment (*Luftgau-Nachrichten-Regiment 1*), which in turn was part of the 1st Air Fleet (*Luftflotte 1*) which served in the theatre of operations of Army Group North. A powerful "Freya" radar had been set up in Vzvad to support the airfield at Staraya Russa, the base for one of the three groups of the *"Grünherz"* fighter wing (JG 54) of *Luftflotte 1*, specifically the second group (the other two were stationed at the airfields of Siwerskaya and Krasnowardeisk). This airfield also provided occasional services to other transport and bomber units of *Luftflotte 1*.

The exact type of the "Freya" radar set used at Vzvad is not known, but it was operated by specialist troops of the 6th Radio Company of the 1st Signals Regiment (*6./1.Lg-Nr-Reg*). Whichever type it was, it was designed to use radio wave pulses to detect far away air targets (at that time the range was around 70 km and the

operating ceiling 12,000 metres) and locate their position; in other words, distance and bearing (azimuth and delay). The "Freya" provided information when the optical systems failed (due to bad weather or at night) and at a greater distance than sound locators. This information was vital to the 16th Army's air cover since it enabled interceptor fighters to be deployed and anti-aircraft artillery (or Flak) to be guided.

Once the Vzvad Support Point had been lost on 20 January 1942, the *Luftwaffe* would install a Würzburg radar at the Staraya Russa airfield. It was a less effective system than the "Freya" radar.

Fig.6
Abb. 6
Armazón giratorio en posición de fun-
Drehstand in Betriebsstellung cionamiento

SUBDIVIDED DEPLOYMENT OF THE 81st INFANTRY DIVISION, JANUARY 1942

The splitting up of the 81st Infantry Division is evidence of the functional versatility of German commanders when faced with tactical problems, and the dramatic shortage of reserves available to Army Group North, and by extension to the *Wehrmacht*, in the crisis of January 1942.

The division, which had previously been employed as a garrison unit in France, was urgently sent to Russia. Its participation in the campaign in the west had been limited; it took part in no major battles. In short it was an unblooded unit, mostly equipped with Czech made war materiel. For this reason it was thought that it would be better to use its regiments to reinforce other units, rather than assign the division to its own combat zone. Following normal German practice, mixed *Kampfgruppen* (Combat Groups) were formed with elements of the division. Each group was basically made up of one of the division's infantry regiments and one of its light howitzer groups. However, the serious penetration of the front defended by the 126th Infantry Division would make it necessary to redeploy two of these artillery groups.

Badge of the 81st Infantry Division.

1st COMBAT GROUP. Sent to the II Army Corps sector, at the extreme south-western end of Army Group North, although later it would end up in Toropets, under the command of Army Group Centre, where it would be annihilated some weeks later:

- 189th Infantry Regiment in its entirety.
- II Group of the 181st Light Artillery Regiment (the Division's artillery regiment).
- Staff and 3rd Company 181st Sappers.
- 2nd and 3rd Transport Columns.

2nd COMBAT GROUP. On its way from France it passed through Novgorod, being assigned to the XXXIX Army Corps, part of the 18th Army, in the Chudovo zone, to the north of Novgorod:

- 161st Infantry Regiment (Staff and Battalions I and III).
- 2nd Company of 181st Sappers.
- III Group of the 181st Light Artillery Regiment (as from 15 January it was under the orders of the XXXVIII Army Corps, in the 126th Division sector).

Model 1930 gas mask with M38 canister used by the first contingent of the Blue Division in 1941 and by all other similar units of the Wehrmacht. It is a complete matching set, unaltered since its manufacture. The entire set – mask, straps, filter, canister, lenses – is stamped with the year 1940. (Luis Camacho Fenet)

3rd COMBAT GROUP. According to the original plan, it should have been deployed in the Blue Division's sector, but in response to strategic developments it was transferred to the X Army Corps, Staraya Russa sector, with *General* Schopper at its head:

• General Staff 81st Division.
• 174th Infantry Regiment in its entirety.
• II Battalion of the 161st Infantry Regiment.
• I Group of the 181st Light Artillery Regiment (it never reached Staraya Russa but instead was diverted to fill the breach opened up in the line defended by the 126th Division).
• Signals and 1st Company of 181st Sappers.

REMAINDER OF THE 81ST DIVISION UNITS. Subordinate to the XXXVIII Army Corps, they were being used where needed in various sectors.

• IV Group 181st Heavy Artillery Regiment.
• 181st Reconnaissance Squadron.
• 181st Anti-Tank Group.
• 1st Transport Column.
• Rearguard troops not forming part of the combat groups.

The weight behind the Soviet attack prevailed, and the hopes that Von Chappuis had placed in the 81st Division were dashed in a matter of hours. To his dismay, not only was the Blue Division not relieved by the 81st as he had wished, and not only would he lose the scant reserves he thought he would have, which *General* Busch had decided to send to various other sectors, but he also suffered the ignominy of having to call on the Spanish, whom he had so unfairly maligned, to help him and his XXXVIII Army Corps stem the debacle which was beginning to unfold at the front defended by his 126th Division. Chappuis's dismay was heightened by the equally unpleasant surprise that, to the south of Lake Ilmen, the neighbouring X Army Corps was receiving support from a Spanish Ski Company.

Apart from Vzvad and other positions to the north of the 290th Infantry Division which were being overrun by Morozov's men, the largest concentration of German troops was to be found in the strategic communications and supply centre of Staraya Russa. Its defence was the responsibility of *Colonel* Werner von Erdmannsdorff, commander of the 30th Regiment of the 18th Motorized Division.

The second improvised combat group of the 81st Infantry Division began to descend on Staraya Russa, with *General* Schopper and his General Staff at

German garrison troops on the banks of the Ilmen, in the first winter on the Russian Front. (AHSR)

German tank to the south of Lake Ilmen in August 1941. (AHSR)

the head. It consisted of the Anti-Tank Group of the 18th Motorized Infantry Division (which had been licking its wounds to the rear of the Blue Division after the terrible mauling it had taken in the offensive and subsequent retreat to Tikhvin), several battalions of Field Gendarmerie (the 561st, and later the 319th and the 27th), plus the 16th Auxiliary Police Battalion (*Schuma-Bataillon*) of Latvian volunteers. Hansen also ordered the Reconnaissance Battalion of the 3rd SS *Totenkopf* Division to the town of Staraya Russa, thus escaping the Demyansk encirclement where the rest of this SS Division would be trapped).

GERMAN INFANTRY EQUIPMENT, RUSSIAN FRONT, WINTER OF 1941/1942
(LUIS CAMACHO FENET COLLECTION)

PHOTO I

- P08 "Luger" pistol with holster. Manufactured by DWM (*Deutsche Waffen und Munitionsfabriken*). Used in both world wars.
- Two belt buckles of the *Heer* painted in *Feldgrau* grey: the aluminium one made in 1939 by *Overhoff & Cie* and the steel one made in 1941 by *Berg und Nolte*, both companies based in Lüdenscheid.
- M40 helmet with single decal. Marked "EF64", indicating that it was made by *Emaillierwerk, AG*, at Fulda, size 64. The chin strap is marked 1941.
- M40 infantry epaulettes (white *Waffenfarbe*) for privates and corporals.
- Breast eagle for the M40 *Feldbluse* (field tunic) and later models, in its original fabric.
- *"Oberschütze"* (senior rifleman) badge for the *Feldbluse* M40 and later models.
- Bayonet for the Mauser Kar 98k rifle with its frog and belt. Matching serial number, make and year for bayonet and frog, 41ffc for *"Friedrich Abr. Herder und Sohn"*, Solingen, 1941. Serial number 3843e. The bayonet and its sheath belonged to a soldier of the Blue Division.
- M31 Canteen (1942) and M31 bread bag (unmarked, but it is very probably an example from 1941-42).
- Pack of bandages for the inside first aid pocket of the *Feldbluse*. Dated 1939.

PHOTO 2

- Ribbon bar with two ribbons, one for the War Merit Cross with Swords and the other for the Winter Campaign in the East Medal.
- Assault infantry badge, in silver. Marked "M.K.1." for the manufacturer "Metalle & Kunststoffe" of Gablonz.
- Iron Cross 1st Class. Not marked, but clearly an example attributable to the manufacturer "B.H. Mayer" of Pforzheim.
- Wound medal, in black. Unmarked.
- DRL (*Deutsches Reichsabzeichen für Leibesübungen*) sports badge in bronze, made by Werstein-Jena.

FELDBLUSE M40

- Infantry soldier's M40 *Feldbluse* with 1939 type breast eagle. It's an example issued at the Stettin depot in 1941.
- Dyed black leather combat belt with a steel buckle, unmarked and undated. Used as from 1940.

BLUE DIVISION OBJECTS RESCUED FROM THE VOLKHOV FRONT, 1941-42 (JAIME SADURNÍ COLLECTION)

- Spanish helmets found on the Volkhov Front.
- Zinc dogtag (10th Company 262nd Regiment) found at Spaskaja Polist (Volkhov Pocket).
- Aluminium dogtag (2nd Anti-Tank Company) found at Kopzy with blood type "O".
- Infantry belt buckle found at Tyutitsy.
- Falangist badge found at Teremetz (displayed with an SEU badge, a Blue Division badge, contemporary press cuttings and documents, and two original *Wehrmacht* medals).

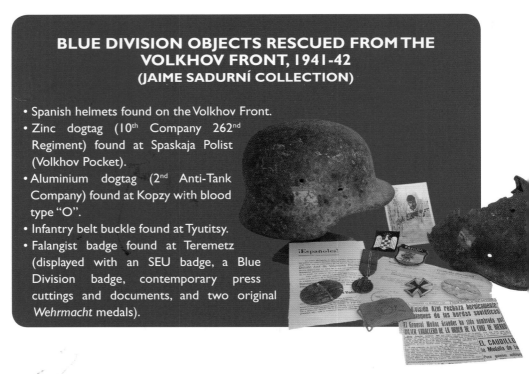

Unposed photo of two guards facing the Soviet enemy lines. (Authors' collection)

Meanwhile reinforcements were arriving, and Vzvad was overrun by advance units of Soviet skiers equipped with snowploughs and motorized sleds. Hansen, using the ragbag collection of units under his command, tried to hold the enemy far from Staraya Russa. On the low ground flanking the River Redya, a tributary of the River Lovat, he positioned a number of companies of the 502nd Infantry Regiment (290th Infantry Division) and the 30th Motorcycle Rifle Battalion (20th Motorized Infantry Division). Resistance was minimal in the face of a number of KV-1 tanks of the 8th Tank Brigade of the 11th Army. With the German outpost line lost, a second line of defence was established between the villages of Anuchino and Sloboda, manned by II Battalion, 501st Regiment (290th Division), I Battalion, 26th Regiment (30th Division), and several platoons of sappers. On 10 January the bulk of the 8th Tank Brigade and a large amount of artillery broke through the line defended by I Battalion, 26th Regiment, which forced the entire force to fall back on Staraya Russa.

On 11 January, four days after the start of the offensive, Morozov had positioned the 182nd and 84th Rifle Divisions in front of Staraya Russa. *Colonel* Erdmannsdorff organized the mishmash of forces under his command, a total of 6,500 men, into a makeshift but determined defence. A third of them, *Luftwaffe*, railway and TODT Organization men, formed a second line while the battle line was made up of the five battalions of Infantry and the SS *Totenkopf* Reconnaissance Battalion, which formed up in the eastern sector, the most exposed part of the town's defensive line. In terms of artillery they could muster twenty-eight cannons of various calibres (two of 10 cm, thirteen of 10.5 cm, fourteen of 15 cm, and two 21 cm mortars) plus a battery of four 88 mm anti-aircraft cannons.

GERMAN MOUNTAIN LIGHT INFANTRY
(*GEBIRGSJÄGER*)

The Ski Company of the Blue Division was a small unit in a classic infantry division without any special training. Nevertheless, its men, and especially those who took part in the epic Lake Ilmen episode, saw themselves as a shock or elite unit and liked to be thought of as the equivalent of German *Gebirgsjäger* mountain light infantry (hence the use of the edelweiss flower badge) although the similarity was remote.

The origin of the German mountain troops harks back to 1915 during the Great War. The *Gebirgsjäger* distinguished themselves in combat, led by competent officers (the famous Erwin Rommel among them). A group of these troops was maintained during the Weimar Republic, but it was Hitler's arrival in power and the start of German rearmament which boosted the mountain unit's importance. The *Wehrmacht* formed as many as eight mountain divisions, including one of skiers, in addition to other less important units.

The *Gebirgsjäger* were light infantry troops trained for mountain combat. They mainly fought as assault infantry, a role they were particularly adept at, largely due to their extraordinary physical condition (they were used to climbing mountains carrying a considerable amount of kit).

The light green piping on their rank insignia and certain items of uniform, the use of mountain boots, and the cloth patches on their sleeves, representing the edelweiss flower, identified these seasoned German mountain troops.

1. German mountain light infantry being trained in combat in winter conditions and in the use of skis. (Private collection)

2. Edelweiss flower badge. (Private collection)

3. Epaulette of an *Oberfeldwebel* (sergeant) serving in the 137th Regiment of Mountain Light Infantry. (Authors' collection)

4. In May 1940, during the invasion of Norway, around 200 *Gebirgsjäger* were trained as paratroopers and were later dropped in the outskirts of Narvik in order to reinforce *General* Dietl's men, who were under pressure from the Allies. These men proudly wore their parachutist badge on their uniforms. (Private collection)

5. *Gebirgsjäger* in a propaganda postcard of the period. (Private collection)

6. *Gebirgsjäger* at rest. (Private collection)

7. German *Bergschuhe*, mountain boots with the double-thick soles and metal studs and rivets typical of mountain light infantry troops. (Private collection)

8. Edelweiss flower arm badge belonging to a survivor of the Spanish Ski Company. This hand embroidered patch was introduced in 1939 and worn by officers and troops of *Gebirgsjäger* units. (Authors' collection)

9. Badge of the Collective Military Medal with the edelweiss flower, awarded to members of the Ski Company. (Luis Miguel Sánchez Pérez)

10. On the Eastern Front, a Soviet prisoner is attended by a comrade while two German mountain light infantrymen look on. (Private collection)

1. Three *Gebirgsjäger* give us a detailed view of their studded mountain boots. (Private collection)

2. German mountain light infantrymen enjoying leave. We can see their distinctive items of clothing: cap, edelweiss, and mountain boots. (Private collection)

3. *Gebirgsjäger* with skis. Note the *Bergmütze*, the characteristic mountain cap worn by mountain troops, with a high crown and a short visor. Also visible are the Black Wound Badge, the Infantry Assault Badge, and the Narvik Battle Shield. (Bundesarchiv)

On 12 January the 84th Division cut the railway line and the road to Dno and was able to reach the outskirts of Staraya Russa from the west. The town, now completely surrounded, began to be bombarded by artillery. By nightfall the following day the forceful response from the Germans had succeeded in ousting from the town limits (and destroying) the Soviet 382nd Rifle Regiment, albeit at the cost of a considerable number of casualties.

The total encirclement was maintained until 15 January when reinforcements sent by *General* Busch succeeded in reopening communications with Dno. The three battalions of the 174th Infantry Regiment, supported by several batteries, used their firepower to good effect. They cleared the road to Dno and were soon able to embrace the defenders of Staraya Russa.

Despite a tentative attempt to relieve it, the besieged Vzvad garrison, now cut off from the 290th Division and initially under the tactical command of the 18th Motorized Division by orders from Hansen, was abandoned to its fate. Pröhl and his men rejected a call to surrender made by the enemy and braced themselves for what was to be a relentless artillery battering alternating with attacks by the 140th Rifle Regiment. The Soviet infantry were supported by tanks, one of which would receive two direct hits from one of the anti-tank guns deployed to the south of Vzvad.

As the days went by, any hope of outside help arriving by land proved to be in vain. Staraya Russa was having a hard enough time defending itself without rescuing Vzvad. Casualties were frequent and provisions started to run out; horses were slaughtered to feed the men. To protect themselves against the cold the Germans stripped Russian corpses of their outer clothing. From the air the

Infantry of Army Group North in the first winter of war. (Via authors)

Luftwaffe dropped containers with provisions, ammunition and a number of medals: the Knight's Cross of the Iron Cross for *Captain* Pröhl, five Iron Crosses First Class and twenty Iron Crosses Second Class for the defenders who had most distinguished themselves, including *Lieutenant*s Matthis and Beisinghof, *Sergeant*s Matzen and Feuer, and others. In addition, a *Fieseler Storch* aircraft dropped one Doctor Günther off in Vzvad, with bandages, medical instruments and supplies. Hitler was apprised of the siege and urged the defenders to hold on. We will be returning to Vzvad later.

While Combat Group Pröhl (*Kampfgruppe Pröhl*) fulfilled its role at Vzvad - which was to slow down the enemy advance - the fighting around Staraya Russa continued unabated. The town was still semi-encircled and the importance of the area to the north, between the town and Lake Ilmen, grew as it represented a possible corridor through which the Russians could penetrate into the heart of the 16th Army's rearguard. Here the recently arrived units, amongst which was the Ski Company of the Blue Division, enabled the Germans to operate in force with a view to establishing a line of containment against the 11th Soviet Army.

ERICH HERMANN SCHOPPER

Erich Hermann Schopper was born on 2 July 1892 in Zeulenroda, Turingia, into a well-off family (his father, Ferdinand, was a businessman). In 1912 he joined the Prussian Army, serving in the 74th Artillery Regiment. In 1913 he was promoted to Second Lieutenant, fighting with this rank in the Great War in the aforementioned unit and in the 98th Artillery Regiment. He was awarded both Iron Crosses and, after the Treaty of Versailles, he remained in the *Reichswehr*, in the 6th Artillery Regiment. As colonel of this unit at the outbreak of the Second World War he took part in the Western Campaign and in the occupation of France. He took command of the 81st Infantry Division, fighting on the Russian Front from December 1941 to July 1944 when he was transferred to the Brigade Staff of the 310th Artillery Division for "special missions" (this division, like other similar divisions formed on the Eastern Front in 1944, had no organizational units other than the aforementioned Brigade Staff). He saw out the remainder of the war in the 310th Division, having been awarded the German Cross in Gold (26 December 1941) and the Knight's Cross (30 April 1943). He died in Minden on 18 August 1978.

By early February 1942 the battle to the south of Lake Ilmen was over. Morozov was unable to take German-held Staraya Russa and his concerns were now the same as those of Berzarin's 34th Army. Towards the south-east Morozov's 202nd, 254th and 26th divisions had all but destroyed the German 290th and 30th divisions, penetrating deeply towards the south and so circling around the back of the bulk of the 3rd SS *Totenkopf* Division. And further to the south-east, the 34th Soviet Army had succeeded in defeating the German II Army Corps, which was forced to withdraw to the area of Demyansk. A little later, as we have already related, the two German pockets of Demyansk and Cholm were created. Thus by keeping Staraya Russa in German hands, among other factors, these two pockets were able to survive long enough to be relieved some months later.

The will to resist of the Russian soldier, suitably reinforced by Russia's own propaganda, increased with the Red Army's counter-offensive launched in December 1941. (Authors' collection)

VASILY I. MOROZOV

Morozov was born in 1897 and fought in the Tsarist Army before joining the Red Army. He was trained at the Frunze military academy and during the interwar period he commanded three different infantry divisions and two army corps. His vast experience in the command of infantry units made him the right man for the job of leading a frontline unit such as the 11th Army from June 1941 to November 1942 (thanks to his expertise this army was skilfully able to withdraw through Lithuania and Latvia during the early stages of the German invasion). The 11th Army shouldered the burden of the offensive that this book deals with, but it was unable to capture any of its objectives. In November 1942, Morozov was placed in command of the Soviet First Shock Army, but after 1943 he was removed from the battlefront and given instruction and training duties in Moscow. He died in 1964.

3

Creation and Deployment of the 250th Ski Company of the Blue Division

We now go back to November 1941 when the Staff of Army Group North, expecting the winter campaign to be a drawn out affair, ordered the creation of companies of skiers in each infantry division. The aim was to provide each division with an autonomous, mobile, and flexible unit capable of fulfilling any task required of it in battle. On 22 November 1941, the 250th Division, following orders from the XXXVIII Army Corps, began to organize a ski company. A few days later their commander made it clear that *"it's not a case of proposing solutions that are impractical under current conditions, but rather of achieving practical results by making use of all the resources at our disposal."*

It is impossible to tell the full story of the 250th Ski Company, created on the fly at this very battle front, because no operations log survives. During the first few months of the company's life it is very likely that no such log even existed. Being an *ad hoc*

The Spanish soldiers of the Ski Company were completely immune to Soviet propaganda. (Authors' collection)

unit its history was precarious; in fact for a long time its members continued to be attached to their original units for administrative purposes. Nevertheless we can reconstruct the main events affecting the Ski Company leading up to the heroic action at Lake Ilmen.

The men of the new unit were chosen among volunteers of various combat units and services who, whenever possible, knew how to ski or skate. Some adventurers and men who did not fit in with other units also ended up in the Ski Company. Most came from the Artillery Regiment and the 262nd and 263rd Infantry Regiments (but not the 269th, which was very understrength). There were also thirteen volunteers from the Transport Group and eleven from the Medical Group, several of the latter from the National Sports Delegation of the SEU in Madrid who had experience in sports.

In his diary the Falangist Secretary General of the SEU, José María Gutiérrez del Castillo, wrote about the recruitment from his unit, the

In the centre, Luis Lorenzo Salgado, of the 250th Ski Company, in Riga recovering from the wounds received on 1 December 1941. To his left is Emilio Martí and to his right Dionisio Porres Gil, a journalist and ex-combatant of the Civil War (where he served as a provisional officer), who at the time was editor-in-chief of *Hoja de Campaña*, the Blue Division's own newspaper. (Virgilio Hernández Rivadulla)

1st Ambulance Platoon: *"23 November 1941, Sunday: I have had maybe the worst day of my life, because the Lieutenant [Castañer], Virgilio, Salgado, Piernavieja and Covisa have gone off to the battalion [sic] of skiers; I was all torn up inside. I wanted to go with them but I can't ski..."*

Spanish skiers in December 1941, next to a windmill in the Lake Ilmen sector. (Guillermo González de Canales)

Sub-machine gun MP40 (*Maschinenpistole* 40), standard Blue Division issue. In total 996 guns of this type were issued to the first contingent of the Blue Division in the summer of 1941, some of which were used by the Ski Company. However, the example in the photo corresponds to the year 1943. It is marked with the manufacturer's code and year of manufacture, "ayf 43", the manufacturer being Erfurter Maschinenfabrik B. Geipel GmbH (ERMA) and the year 1943. It also bears the serial number "1289u" and the letters "cnd" (the code of the sub-contractor, Krupp-National-Registrierkassen, GmbH, Berlin). (Luis Camacho Fenet)

Lieutenant Jacinto Velasco del Val, recruited in Valladolid and originally in the IV Artillery Group; he took part in the Battle of Lake Ilmen, being wounded on 19 January 1942. In this photo he appears with the insignia of a *Second Lieutenant* in the *Wehrmacht* although his rank in the Spanish Army at the time was *Provisional Lieutenant* of the *FET y de los JONS* Militia. He recovered from his wounds and when the campaign was over he joined the Military Office Corps. (José Enrique Usunáriz Mocoroa)

The officer who took command of the company, as the most senior of the seven officers in the unit, was *Artillery Lieutenant* José Otero de Arce, previously serving in the 7th Battery. He immediately set about organizing the unit, moving to the north-west bank of the Ilmen. He first went to Staroya Rakoma, home of the sector headquarters, where the Blue Division Exploration Group had set up their command post in a Russian orthodox chapel. Later he moved to Novoye Rakomo, a village 200 metres from the banks of the lake where the company's depot and, initially at least, its command post were sited. For operational and logistical purposes the Ski Company reported to the Exploration Group whose commander was *Major* Ángel Sánchez del Águila Menco; *Lieutenant* Otero de Arce received his orders from this officer.

LIEUTENANT OTERO DE ARCE
The driving force of the Ski Company

José Otero de Arce was born in Buenos Aires on 2 March 1917, the son of José Otero Pazos and Emilia de Arce Campo, emigrants from the Spanish region of Galicia. His father was a businessman working in the province of Salta in Argentina. At an early age he returned to Spain with his parents and brothers, Luis and Celso. The family set up home on a plot of land they owned in Chantada (Lugo) and José, after attending a school in La Coruña, went on to study Chemistry at Santiago de Compostela University.

When the rebellion broke out against the Frente Popular, he traded his books for arms and enlisted in the Falangist militia in Lugo. On 20 July 1936 he went to war, setting out from the barracks of the 30th Infantry Regiment Zaragoza. At the head of a squad of volunteers with the column of *Major* Santos, he occupied Ponferrada before heading south to Castile with *Lieutenant-Colonel* Nevado de Bouza's column. During the summer he saw active service at Alto de los Leones before returning to Lugo in September where, after a brief trial period as a sailor on the heavy cruiser *Canarias*, he joined the *Bandera Legionaria* (Legion Battalion) of the provincial Falange. Until November 1937, first as a provisional *second lieutenant* and then as a provisional *lieutenant,* he served on the Leon Front in various batteries of the 16th Light Artillery Regiment.

After the fall of Asturias he was sent to the I Mountain Artillery Group (105 mm howitzers) of the 81st Division. With this unit, serving in the Staff and as adjutant, he took part in the battles of Teruel and Levante, acquitting himself with distinction in the engagements of Vértice Salada and Peña Juliana in the mountains of El Toro in July 1938, and also in the Battle of Peñarroya-Pueblonuevo in Extremadura in the final weeks of the conflict, in January 1939.

General José Otero de Arce's medals and badges.

1st ROW- 1. A pair of artillery collar badges, regulation uniform 1943 •2. Spanish War Cross, mod. 1942 (for officers and NCOs) •3. Red Cross of Military Merit (for officers and NCOs), with four repeat bars (5 awards) •4. 1936-1939 Campaign Medal (vanguard) •5. Suffering for the Motherland Medal with wound cross embroidered on the ribbon •6. Iron Cross 1st Class, mod. 1957 (Germany) •7. Iron Cross 2nd Class (Germany) •8. Russian Campaign Medal (Spain) •9. 1941/1942 Winter Campaign in the East Medal (Germany) •10. Commemorative Medal for Spanish Volunteers in the Struggle against Bolshevism (Germany) •11. A pair of general staff collar badges, regulation uniform 1943 •12. War School Badge (Italy)

2nd ROW- 13. Central Staff Badge, regulation uniform 1943 •14. General Staff College Badge (for generals, commanders, officers, and assistant teachers that have been in their post for two years without interruption) •15. Spanish War Cross, mod. 1942, two awards (for commanders) •16. Seagull badge (from his stay in Italy) •17. Black Wound Badge (Germany) •18. Individual Military Medal with Lake Ilmen ribbon bar, 24-1-1942 •19. Medal bar of miniature medals. •20. Infantry Assault Badge in silver (Germany) •21. Badge of the ISMI: *Istituto Stati Maggiori Interforze* (Italy). •22. Badge of the Higher General Staff Course, for officers of the armed forces (Italy)

3rd ROW- 23. Badge for the teaching staff of the Higher Army School •24. Badge for time served on the teaching staff, with service bars (gold, 5 years: blue, 10 years). •25. Badge for attending the Course in Detection and Location of Targets (created in 1961) •26. Badge for Specialists in Logistics •27. Artillery collar badges, regulation uniform 1943 (Brigadier General)

4th ROW- 28. Cross of Military Merit with white distinctive, for commanders (1st Class) •29. Medal of the Order of Saint Hermenegild •30. Grand Cross of the Order of Saint Hermenegild (mod. post-1979) •31. Cross of the Order of Saint Hermenegild (mod. 1951) •32. Sahara Medal (Central Administration ribbon) •33. War Cross for Military Valour, mod. 1922 (Italy) •34. Cross of the Order of Merit (Italy) •35. Order of the Cross of the Eagle 3rd Class with Swords (Germany) •36. Brigadier General's insignia.

In July 1941 he joined the Blue Division in Ceuta from Laucién (Morocco) where he had been stationed with the 49th Artillery Regiment. He entered the 7th Battery of the Blue Division Artillery Regiment which, on arrival at the front, was deployed on the island of Novgorod. He served as an officer on the gun line and at forward observation posts, and his battery supported the actions of the 262nd Regiment. His eagerness to fight led him to request a transfer to the new Ski Company, of which he was appointed commander. His was the brain behind its organization and preparation for the battle of Lake Ilmen in which he acted as second-in-command under the orders of *Captain* Ordás. Otero was always in the front line of all operations before finally falling victim to frostbite at the end of the engagement.

By 4 March 1942 he was back in command of the Ski Company. On 18 April the unit joined the line in the Podberesje sector on the edge of the Volkhov Pocket and Otero fought with distinction in repelling several enemy attacks. He continued his Russian campaign at the head of his unit until he handed his command over on 25 July, having been granted home leave in Spain. When he returned in September the Company had a new commander (José María Gómez de Salazar y Nieto), so Otero was given command of the 2nd Platoon which he led in the Battle of Krasny Bor, among other actions. The Battle of Krasny Bor left his unit in tatters, so he was transferred to the Field Gendarmerie where he took charge of the Troop Section. He held this post until June 1943 when he left the front to serve in the Representation of the Blue Division in Berlin. He remained in the capital of the *Reich* until his repatriation

As Commander of the 250th Ski Company during the Russian campaign.

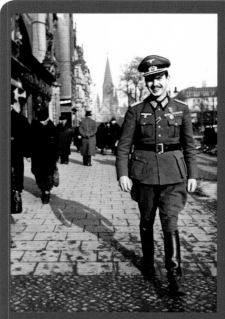

In Berlin, serving in the Representation of the Blue Division.

in October 1943, after a campaign lasting over two years. Some months later he enrolled on a course at the Military Transformation Academy in Segovia. It is interesting to note that, unlike *Captain* Ordás, who received his Individual Military Medal immediately, Otero had to wait until 1948 before being awarded his in recognition of his conduct at Lake Ilmen.

Having been promoted by seniority to artillery captain, on 25 November 1945 he married his fiancée of eight years, María Luisa Muerza Anzoaín from Navarre (one of her cousins was José Miguel Muerza, a fighter pilot with Morato's 'Blue Patrol'). The couple would have four children: José Luis (†), Carlos José, María Luisa, and José Javier. During Otero's Russian campaign his then fiancée, María Luisa, anxiously waited at her home in Madrid, in Conde de Peñalver Street. Not only did she never fail to write to him every day, but on her way to morning mass at the Cristo de Medinaceli Basilica she maintained a vow of silence in exchange for his safe return.

After obtaining his Military Staff Diploma, Otero de Arce served in various artillery units but soon sought a more permanent position in Madrid, which he alternated with stays abroad; in Italy, where he spent two years at the Civitavecchia War School, between 1955 and 1957, and in the UK and Ireland, where he served as military attaché at the Spanish embassies in London and Dublin, respectively. On his promotion to colonel in 1971 he was sent to the Canary Islands to the Staff of the 2nd Troop Command and the *Gran Canaria* Troop Command. His final posting was as a military educator, a role very close to his heart, as head of studies in the Higher Army School. He retired from service in April 1979, shortly after being promoted to Brigadier General.

Promoted to *Artillery Brigadier General* in 1971.

His panoply of medals, insignia and badges is testimony to his dedication to Spain and the Army. On a more personal level we would highlight the many foreign languages he spoke (French, English, German, Italian and Portuguese) and also his artistic and cultural side, expressed in such diverse fields as painting and music (he played the piano, the guitar, and the accordion), cooking, and stamp collecting. He was very much a family man, a father figure even. His summer holidays were always split between San Adrián, Navarre, where his wife was from, and a beach resort. A congenial man and a good conversationalist, he was not given to talking about war. In family gatherings he would tell stories about his campaigns simply, without embellishment, avoiding any references to heroism. Every three months he used to meet up with a group of friends of the Blue Division at the Cafetería Manila, in Madrid's Serrano Street, some of them fellow combatants of the Battle of Lake Ilmen. He died in Cadiz on 18 November 1980, on his way to the Canary Islands.

The Ski Company's initial strength, a little over 150 men, was complemented by more volunteers who trickled in to that remote place from wherever their original units were stationed. By early December 1941 the company could muster 212 men: seven officers, fourteen sergeants, and the rest troopers. In addition to the Staff headed by *Lieutenant* Otero de Arce, and in coordination with the Blue Division's headquarters, six platoons were organized, led by *Lieutenants* Vicente Castañer Enseñat, Antonio García Porta and Jacinto Velasco del Val, and *Second Lieutenants* Germán Bernabéu del Amo, Joaquín García Larios, and Alfonso López de Santiago.

Although the photo is overexposed and of poor quality, it is worth publishing. It was taken in Babki at New Year 1942, and features a number of the Company's men (many who were later to perish) posing with some of the local population. From left to right, Virgilio Hernández Rivadulla, Manuel Herreros Granado, Mariano Barbasán Larrea (†), a "*mamushka*" with two "*malenkis*", *Second Lieutenant* Joaquín García Larios (†), *Corporal* Manuel Muñoz Simón (†), and Guillermo Ruiz Gijón. (Guillermo González de Canales)

The Company had a surprisingly large number of platoons, more than in a rifle company which normally had three (albeit with up to three squads), and lacked any heavy armament. The Company only had one sub-machine gun (machine pistol in Spanish parlance) per platoon; no mortars and not even one machine gun. The reason behind this atypical composition and the lack of any of the supporting weaponry with which you would expect infantry to be equipped lies in the type of mission the Company was entrusted with; the surveillance and patrolling of the banks of Lake Ilmen. The unit's fighting capability relied on manoeuvrability – which is why they were equipped with skis –, rather than firepower. In short it was a light infantry unit, not equipped for combat per se, but intended for reconnaissance and rapid response if necessary.

The Company was deployed to the extreme south of the Blue Division's disposition, spanning a string of villages on the bank of the lake, several of which had previously been occupied by the 3rd Anti-Tank Company: Kuchinovo, Samokrazha, Babki, Lukinchino, Nogolovo, Morino, and Spasspiskopez. The unit's Staff was stationed first in Babki and later in Spasspiskopez. This deployment of the Ski Company, together with other companies of the Exploration Group and the Anti-Tank Group, can be explained by the idiosyncrasy of this type of unit.

All of them formed part of the "motorized echelon" of the Blue Division. Being deployed defensively, their true role as an offensive and reconnaissance unit lost tactical importance and they were relegated to the Division's reserve. In offensive mode the marching order was Exploration Group first with the Anti-Tank Group following up, but at that time, late in November 1941, the 250th Division's line of contact with the enemy, apart from the Volkhov Bridgehead (which had just three weeks left to survive), was located on Volkhov Island and along the course of the river. In these sectors the Russian pressure was much more intense and, to some extent, Lake Ilmen was considered as a relatively quiet zone, although it still needed to be properly watched.

Ilmen, December 1941. The 3rd Anti-Tank Company of *Captain* Ordás posing together with the Ski Company. (Jesús Zaera León family collection)

SERGEANT LEANDRO POLANCO Y DRAKE

Sergeant Polanco of the Staff of the Ski Company, wearing his Iron Cross awarded on 31 January 1942. On his return from the campaign he married María Eugenia Esquíroz García (with whom he would have two children). She was the sister of Fernando, an "Old Guard" (pre-Civil War Falangist) of the Madrid 269th Regiment, who was wounded at Posselok on 12 November 1941 and died two days later in Possad. Leandro Polanco was also a cousin of the Blue Division combatant brothers, *Lieutenant* Luis Polanco Mejorada and *Private* Ernesto Polanco Mejorada. Leandro, who went on to have two children, worked for the Port Workers' Organization of the Ministry of Labour and died in Madrid, on 8 December 1980. (Archive of Carlos Esquíroz Gaumé)

The sector guarded by the Ski Company, in line with and to the north of the Anti-Tank Group units, was about eight kilometres long. Each platoon usually took over one of the villages, billeting its squads in the homes of the local population, mostly women, children and old people, since any young male of military age had been recruited by the Red Army.

The skiers acclimatized themselves to the truly Arctic weather of the area around the lake. Morale and spirits were high. There was no shortage of volunteers for the gruelling outdoor guard duties, even for night watches (which could never last much longer than an hour because of the risk of fatal hypothermia). Guillermo González de Canales describes in his diary the guard duty he endured on the night of his birthday, 6 December 1941:

"On my second watch I had to do 2 to 3 in the morning. The cold was tremendous. There was

"On the parapet, the cold chills to the bone, but the Spanish soldier knows how to grit his teeth and face the enemy." (Blue Division *Hoja de Campaña*, no. 13, Tuesday, 4 February 1942)

a moon that was shrouded a little by the mist off the lake. Instead of coming from the [north] pole as in previous days, the wind was blowing from the north-east, from Siberia, which, oddly enough, is even worse (…). The temperature dropped, my breath froze, and my eyes were red with the ice particles carried by the wind. There was ice on my eyelashes too, which I had to pull off so I could see, and ice crystals on my cheeks. If I spat the saliva made a cracking noise as it froze before hitting the snow, like one shard of glass falling on another. It's horrible! Which enemy is worse? I know that a very short distance away the enemy is moving, armed to the teeth, dressed in white and vastly outnumbering us; we are seven to their fifty at least, and yet this cold, this cold may be far worse (…). If I'm lucky enough to get back I pray to God that I'm not missing my feet, my nose, or my ears. That would be worse than death."

RELATIONS WITH THE LOCAL LAKE ILMEN PEOPLE

Despite the fact that the situation was one of war and that the Blue Division was acting as an occupying military force in the sector, relations between the Ski Company and the other Spanish units deployed in the Ilmen sector with the local populace were human and even warm. The Spanish lived in *izbas* which they shared with the resident families and the two parties were forced to rub along. It was impossible for anyone to be outside for more time than was absolutely essential to perform their respective duties. Long hours were spent indoors and everyone needed to adjust to what were complicated living conditions.

Let us now move to Lukinchino, with Guillermo González de Canales and Ramón Farré Palaus, who write in their diary and memoirs, respectively, about their arrival at this village on 28 November 1941. The former recounts: *"The house we have occupied is hell. It is full of "malenkis" [children] who never stop crying, there is no electricity, it's small, etc., etc. We are hungry. Meals are prepared and we are a little bit happier, but not entirely content because something is missing which is as important for a soldier as food: tobacco."* The latter writes: *"Mother Xura gave me a frosty welcome: she said the house was small and there was nowhere for me to stay, and that there was also an invalid in the house; sure enough, there on a straw mattress lay a blind, half paralyzed old woman. The kids ran riot around the house [she said]. In short it was impossible, and as she said all this she gesticulated wildly, pointing out everything to me and yelling at the top of her voice in a childlike effort to make what she was saying easier for me to understand. It was all to no avail; I said I was staying and I stayed.*" In spite of it all, the Russian (Slavic) and Spanish (Mediterranean) temperaments eventually rubbed along with each other, as Farré Palaus observed: "*It's easy to make friends with the kids; after two days of my being in the house they couldn't be without me (…) Mother Xura also took a shine to me quickly; her original fury subsided to nothing and she looked after me with motherly concern…*"

The *divisionarios* made use of the villagers' firewood and natural resources but shared their provisions with them. The respect for Russian possessions was strict. On one occasion, on 26 November 1941 in Staraya Rakoma, the 1st Platoon of the Ski Company was searched by *Lieutenant* Otero de Arce, looking for a 15th century panel which had apparently been stolen from the local temple. The Russians observed the scene from their houses, to the indignation of some of the volunteers. The officers took action against theft not only in the case of icons; they were similarly strict about the theft of more humble property, such as the much coveted *valenki* [felt-lined boots] which were often pilfered from the locals. One volunteer, Mont Serrano, was obliged to travel to the next village to return a pair of these boots to their rightful owners, after they had been "bought" (i.e requisitioned) for five marks. The *troikas* [sleds] and the *panje* [local horses] used by the Company were similarly restored to their owners once they were no longer needed.

During the month of November nothing worthy of mention happened, with the exception of the spectacular fire which burned down *Lieutenant* Otero de Arce's billet in the afternoon of 30 November.

December would be more eventful. On the night of 1 December two prisoners were captured and in the early hours of the following day, the 1st Platoon of the Company, deployed at Babki under the command of *Lieutenant* Castañer, received a surprise attack. González de Canales, of the first squad, who was warming himself by the stove in his *izba* with his rifle in his hands after having taken the first guard duty, tells us in his diary what happened that night:

"*Suddenly I heard the voice of Valentí* [Ramón Valentí Abadía] *who shouted: 'Attack!' I leapt to his side and before long we both felt our four comrades crawling to our sides. The lake was threatening, long bursts of tracer bullets criss-crossed it from every direction, mostly aimed at where the Lieutenant's shack was.*

VICENTE CASTAÑER ENSEÑAT
Lieutenant of the 1st Platoon of Skiers, survived uninjured

Vicente Castañer Enseñat was born in Inca, Mallorca, on 10 December 1914. The outbreak of the Civil War found him on his home island, where he enlisted in a company of medical corps riflemen under the orders of *Major* Luis Rodríguez Polanco. He later took part in the operations to push *Captain* Bayo's Republican column back into the sea. In September 1938, serving in the 40th Division, in the medical corps, he took part in operations on the Catalonia front (the Segre sector, in Lérida), and also in the battle of Peñarroya in early 1939.

With the rank of non-commissioned[1] lieutenant of the medical corps and stationed with the Galicia Army Corps he volunteered for the Blue Division on 22 July 1941. He was first sent to the 2nd Company, 1st Platoon of the First Ambulance Convoy (Medical Group), but later joined the 1st Platoon of the Ski Company, with which he would cross Lake Ilmen and take part in all subsequent fighting. Between 7 February and 4 March 1942, he took command of the shattered unit in the absence of any other officers. He and his men occupied the blockhouses in the middle of the frozen Lake Ilmen for several days and had a number of encounters with enemy patrols, in which he took two prisoners. Later, once again at the head of his original 1st Platoon, he fought in other sectors.

He was repatriated in October 1942. After retraining as a professional soldier in the Segovia Artillery Academia, in October 1947 he was sent to serve in Artillery Regiment no. 28 (*Santiago de Compostela*) with the rank of captain. He retired from the army the following year and went to live in Valencia where, after a brief period in Bilbao, he remained. He married Guillermina Martorell Suárez in 1945 but had no children. He died with the rank of retired major in Valencia in 1990.

---

1 The Spanish expression "*de complemento*" has been translated as "non-commissioned" although the equivalent is not exact. "*De complemento*" officers are non-career soldiers who have a short-to mid-term contract but can "convert" to being regular, permanent officers by additional training.

Spanish skiers at Nowaja Rakoma towards the end of November 1941. On the left, squatting, is *Corporal* Manuel Muñoz Simón (known as "Ramper"), *Sergeant* Gustavo Sánchez Torres, Ramón Valentí Abadía (with a pipe), Fernando Suárez Pérez and Carlos Urgoiti y Bas (squatting), Guillermo González de Canales (with slung rifle), and behind him, Juan José Mediavilla Fuentes, a medic and another two volunteers (these last three belonging to the Exploration Group). (Guillermo González de Canales)

"We heard a burst of machine pistol (it was Virgilio [Hernández Rivadulla] it jammed on him and he didn't fire any more) and some sporadic rifle shots. Our heads, helmetless, must have been clearly visible above the ice and the snow. Indeed, some 40 paces away we heard shots whistle past us very close. One of these bullets embedded itself in the parapet and another in the spruce post, under our noses. Impatiently I asked Sergeant Gustavo [Sánchez Torres]: 'shall we fire?' He answered no [they went to defend the Lieutenant's izba]. Just then Lieutenant Castañer looked over and when he saw us he said: 'They'll hit you there! Can't you see you're exposed where you are? Get yourselves over there' and he pointed to a shallow trench in the ice where we lay down either side of something bulky, which turned out to be the corpse of poor Torrente [Luis Torrente] who had been shot in the first burst. We rested our feet on him so they wouldn't get cold. He had two bullet wounds, one in the shoulder and another in the head, both fatal…"

At the end of the firefight a tally of casualties was made; one dead, the aforementioned Torrente (the first man killed of the Ski Company) and one wounded, Luis Lorenzo Salgado, hit in the stomach when he went forward to alert *Corporal* Manuel Muñoz's squad. Meanwhile the Russians had two men killed, from whom three guns were retrieved (one a machine gun), two seven-shot revolvers, and twelve hand grenades, not to mention copious "red" propaganda in Spanish. There were also trails of blood in the snow suggesting that there may have been more enemy casualties.

GUILLERMO GONZÁLEZ DE CANALES LÓPEZ
Veteran skier

The son of Fernando González de Canales Romero (his mother's name was Pilar López González de Canales), Guillermo González de Canales was born on 6 December 1915 in Bujalance (Cordoba), where his father was a doctor. Of his five siblings, Alejandro, Patricio, Ramiro, Carlos and Pilar, his brother Patricio achieved a degree of fame due to his public career; he was an "Old Shirt" of the Andalusian Falangist movement and head of its Seville branch, founder and first editor of the newspapers *FE* of Seville and *Alerta* of Santander, and National Secretary for Propaganda of *FET y de los JONS*. He was among the opponents of Franco's Political Unification Decree of April 1937, for which he was arrested by the police. With Narciso Perales he went on to found the legendary and clandestine *Falange Española Auténtica*, an anti-Franquist Falangist organization which, despite having gone through multiple changes, still survives today.

Returning to our Guillermo, he received his first schooling at the Colegio de las Escolapias in Bujalance, Cordoba, and after living a number of years in Marugán (Segovia), where he studied for his high school diploma at home, he moved to Madrid to study at the Veterinary School. The outbreak of the Civil War caught him by surprise in the flat he shared with his brother Ramiro (the flat belonged to his uncle Manuel González de Canales, who was among those shot at Paracuellos del Jarama due to his name having been found on the passenger list of a ship travelling to Rome carrying guests to King Alfonso XIII's wedding). Guillermo was recruited by the People's Republican Army and, since he had attended a course on radiology, he avoided being sent to the front, but instead worked as a radiologist at the war hospital set up in the *Sanatorio de La Fuenfría* TB sanatorium in Cercedilla (Madrid). While he was working at this Republican hospital, one of his "workmates", who knew about his political leanings, told him: *"you, the idle rich, [are here] now because we need you, but later we'll be putting your lot under the ground."* Thankfully he never got the chance. Once the war was over, Guillermo returned to his studies.

In July 1941, he joined the Blue Division "to fight against Communism" and, because he was a trained vet, he was sent to serve with the Animal Butchery Company. Once at the front, on 7 November 1941 he made a written request to transfer to the "Esparza Regiment". As he later wrote: *"When I passed the battleground I saw my dead comrades and so many graves, their heroism, their glory…; I couldn't be separated from them, so I requested a transfer from logistics to infantry."* He ended up in the recently created Ski Company, where he took part in several patrols and in the famous crossing of the lake. After suffering from frostbite he was evacuated to Grigorowo, Porchov and finally Riga, where he remained hospitalized until April 1942. On his return to the front he continued fighting with his company in the Volkhov Pocket and at Novgorod. He kept a methodical diary of his time in the Russian campaign, a source of extraordinary historical value which his family treasures.

On his return from Russia he extended his studies to include human medicine and graduated in Medicine and Surgery, before later specializing in clinical analyses. As a medical analyst he worked in both private medicine and as a vet. He worked at the Madrid municipal laboratory having taken a public competitive exam for the job of veterinary inspector, a post he held until retiring at the age of 70, which he combined with teaching work at the Veterinary School. He married Carmina in 1951 and had three children: Guillermo, María del Pilar and María del Carmen.

A man of profound religious and professional convictions, as a doctor he attended mass for Santa Madre Maravillas de Jesús at Carmelo de la Aldehuela Church on many occasions. He was a man who stood out for his eagerness to learn, his vast knowledge, and his discretion — he always preferred to take a back seat. He was a tireless worker and a compulsive reader. His enormous library contained a large number of books on professional matters, history, and in particular the Falange (he admired José Antonio *"the best man in Spain"* although he did not consider himself to be a *"very active Falangist"*). He was always a great lover of nature and knowledge, and also of his Blue Division; until he died he kept in touch with a group of friends and fellow soldiers of the Ski Company.

The flag of the SEU, the union to which a fair number of the Ski Company volunteers belonged, seen here in a Russia field. (Pepe Guillén Marquina family collection)

Major Sánchez del Águila, head of logistics, as leader of the Ski Company's Exploration Group. To his right is *Major* Homar Servera, serving with the Staff of the Blue Division. (Juan Negreira)

Virgilio Hernández Rivadulla tells how Luis Lorenzo was evacuated:

"I ran to where I'd seen Luis Lorenzo fall as he was coming to help us, and on the way I came across Carlos Urgoiti lying on the ground. Between the two of us we dragged a sled which was on the bank of the lake and lay Luis Lorenzo down in it. With another sled, a horse-drawn one, we took him to the first field telephone [we found] where I got in touch with our old Ambulance Platoon, which sent [an ambulance] immediately. When Urgoiti and I got hold of Luis Lorenzo and loaded him onto the sled, I lifted up

his clothing round his waist and saw the entry wound of the bullet, which I covered with one of the field dressings we all carry with us. When Luis Lorenzo arrived at the hospital at Grigorovo, the surgeon and Doctor Aragón [Medical Lieutenant Emiliano Aragón Treceño], who we all knew since our time in Ambulances, were already ready for him. Later Doctor Aragón told me that the bullet had perforated his intestine in seven places and had grazed his liver, and that he hadn't bled to death because the cold had frozen the entry and exit wounds" (Luis Lorenzo would live to be 96 years old).

GUILLERMO RUIZ GIJÓN
Lawyer, sportsman and veteran of the Ski Company

He was born to parents from Zaragoza and the Levante in Madrid in 1919, in Lope de Vega Street. He spent the Civil War in Valencia, where he was prosecuted and imprisoned for belonging to the SEU. He joined the Blue Division in July 1941 when he was studying Law at Madrid's Central University. Once at the front he requested a transfer from the 10th Company of the 262nd Regiment to the Ski Company. In the fighting on 17 January he was seriously wounded in the leg but recovered "thanks to the intervention of Jesús de Medinaceli", as he liked to remind his family. He continued in the Russian campaign until March 1943.

A born athlete, he formed part of the Spanish hockey team, together with his brother Rafael, at the 1948 London Olympic Games, the same year he married his lifelong girlfriend, Maria Luisa Rodero (also a hockey player). His life was focused on his family, practising law, sport, and politics. He became president of the Spanish Roller Hockey Federation and director of the General Sports Mutual Society. He also devoted a great deal of energy to the National Brotherhood of the Blue Division, of which he was deputy-chairman, and was the legal architect behind the creation of the National Blue Division Foundation. He had four children and died in Madrid on 15 October 2004.

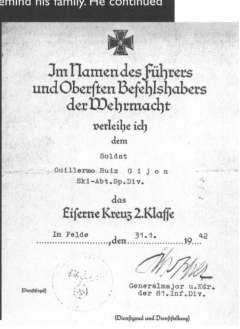

Citation for the Iron Cross 2nd Class.
(Ruiz Gijón family collection)

On the night of 3 December something strange happened. A sentry of the 1st Platoon machine gunned two silhouettes that were approaching his position in the belief they were Russian soldiers. They turned out to be a heavily bearded man and a "girl about 19 years old, well-dressed, very pretty, and with slender, delicate hands". The girl died almost immediately, but not before uttering the word "*nietó*" with a feeble voice. She was buried at dawn, in the presence of a number of Spanish soldiers who had been very upset by the incident. However, some days later a German Lieutenant of the information service came by asking questions about the girl in question. Her body was exhumed and much to the Spanish soldiers' surprise, drawings and documents were found among her clothing. She was a spy…

Defensive position of the Waffen SS with an 81 mm mortar during the first Russian winter. (Via authors)

Soviet riflemen carrying their light machine guns: the perfect image of Russian tenacity in the face of the German invaders. (Za Rodina)

After 18 December 1941, when the Volkhov Bridgehead was abandoned by the Spanish troops, the Russian pressure on the other sectors of the Blue Division intensified. On the lakeside front the Ski Company had to increase its vigilance, placing sentries not only in the villages where its troops were deployed, but also in other small villages without any permanent military garrison. Platoons were sent out to these villages and stood guard for 15 hours, returning to base the following day. The number, reach, and duration of patrols was also stepped up. The soldiers started to suffer from exhaustion from being constantly on the alert.

On 12 December there was another night firefight, this time with partisans in the sector adjoining the one held by the 3rd Anti-Tank Company. For the loss of one Spanish sentry, the anti-tankers and the skiers succeeded in repulsing several waves of attackers, killing four of them. One of them was chased and shot by the *Captain* of the 3rd Anti-Tank Company himself, José Manuel Ordás Rodríguez. The bodies of the enemy dead were examined; they had Tartar features and were well armed and equipped.

THE SOVIET SOLDIER

Soviet commanders never took much care over the welfare of their men. Nevertheless, contrary to the negative and derogatory image created by Axis propaganda, which portrayed Russian soldiers as recalcitrant Bolsheviks, at this stage of the campaign they were experienced troops with proven fighting capabilities.

At Lake Ilmen the Spaniards and their German and Latvian comrades were up against soldiers of Morozov's 11th Army, many of them recruited from Asian Russia beyond the Urals. They were used to the terrain, hardy, accustomed to bivouacking in harsh weather, expert skiers, and liked nothing better than to attack, although they required strong leadership from their officers, which was all too often conspicuous by its absence.

From left to right: Combat Service Medal (2nd type); Order Medal of Glory, 3rd Class (this type began to be awarded later, after 8 November 1943); Medal "For Courage", 2nd type. As in the case of the Combat Service Medal, the regulation ribbon was changed, which means this is the 2nd type. The change of medal type had no effect on award criteria or any other aspect. (Manuel Pérez Rubio)

ÁLVARO MONT SERRANO
A polyfacetic *divisionario:* Falangist, lawyer and musician (cellist)

He was born in Madrid in 1917, the son of the famous trumpeter Álvaro Mont Cañamás (1890-1942), from Albalate de la Ribera (Valencia), and Dolores Serrano. From his father he inherited his passion for music; before the outbreak of the Civil War he played cello in theatre and cinema orchestras while formally studying music. In the light of the unstable political situation, Álvaro decided to anticipate events on 1 May 1936 by joining the anarcho-syndicalist CNT union (a move backed by the Professional Musicians Union, which did nothing to block Álvaro's application), in an attempt to conceal his clear allegiance to the Falange. Thus on 17 July 1936 he was accepted into the CNT. The union always had "a good feeling" about Mont.

The outbreak of the Civil War found him spending the summer in the village of Navalperal de Pinares in the province of Avila. In July 1936 this village of a little over 1,000 inhabitants was the scene of one of the most daring, strange and atypical actions of the start of the conflict: the incursion of *Colonel* Julio Mangada's Republican column behind the lines of the rebel forces. Between 18 and 23 July, Navalperal changed hands on numerous occasions in a mad struggle for possession, which Mont experienced first-hand.

On 25 July, after the village had been occupied by Mangada's forces for two days, Mont jumped in his car – which he had cleverly managed to save from confiscation – and drove to Navas del Marqués to tell the Civil Guard that the bulk of Mangada's column was heading for Villacastín. A small force of no more than 20 Civil Guards approached Navalperal with the idea of retaking it, but were repulsed. During the firefight, Mont and some other combatants took refuge in a nearby pine wood, returning to Navalperal after dark.

On 26 July another group of some 120 men, 80 of them Civil Guards, set out from Avila and this time did succeed in occupying Navalperal de Pinares and Las Navas, initially driving Mangada's meagre column towards Cebreros. But the occupation lasted just a few hours; on the 27th, Mangada's column, reinforced by 600 men, regained control over both villages. A new column of over 100 civil guards and volunteers were powerless to dislodge the well-defended Republican stronghold. Navalperal de Pinares would be in the hands of Popular Front supporters until 8 October 1936.

Mont was unable to join the rebel forces, being irremediably trapped in the village. Under evacuation orders given by Mangada, on 31 July he returned to Madrid where he reported to his union and continued to work as a musician. A year later, on 12 July 1937, he was arrested by agents of the Buenavista police station of the Salamanca district of Madrid. Apparently, he had been informed against by a man named Iglesias, a left-wing sympathizer from Navalperal de Pinares, and by the Local Committee of the same village. Accused of "joining and aiding the rebellion", on 28 October 1937 Mont was tried and convicted by the Special People's Court of Madrid and sentenced to twelve years and a day internment in a labour camp. He served the first few days of his sentence in the Porlier Prison in Madrid (formerly known as Prison no. 3) before being transferred, on 5 November to the Reformatory of Alicante. He was released from prison when the war ended.

His Falangist ideals led him to join the Blue Division where he served in Signals and in the Staff of the Ski Company. Like so many other *divisionarios*, from his time in Russia he would always remember how the civil population were treated. On one occasion, for example, when a fire broke out in an *izba*, several Spanish soldiers, Álvaro among them, entered the burning building to rescue the people inside, one of them an old woman.

On his return from Russia he continued to work in music and the law. He became secretary of the Madrid Symphony Orchestra (by which he was awarded *in memoriam* a Centenary Gold Medal in 2005), and in the field of public law he was head of the Expropriations Department of the General Directorate of Roads of the Ministry of Public Works.

He always kept in touch with his former Blue Division friends and comrades. Every year they hold a mass at the Church of San José, in Alcalá Street, Madrid, in memory of their fallen comrades.

An exceptional husband and father, he died in Madrid on 26 November 2001.

Despite every possible protection, the cold forced Mont to abandon the front with frostbite on 18 January 1942.

Squad of the 250th Ski Company in the summer of 1942, during the Battle of the Volkhov Pocket. From left to right, Álvaro Mont Serrano, Ramón Valentí Abadía, Virgilio Hernández Rivadulla, Guillermo Ruiz Gijón, and one unidentified man. (Mont Serrano family collection)

On the night of 13 December there was an attempt to make a recce towards enemy lines with twenty-five men (ten from Staff and fifteen from the 1st Platoon) under the command of *lieutenant*s Otero de Arce and Castañer. Shortly after setting off towards the lake the order was given to go back, since the Russians, possibly alerted in advance, were sweeping the area with searchlights and sending up flares.

Alarms raised during the night were common, as were firefights. Often men fired into the darkness without knowing who or what they were shooting at. Almost every night the skiers would hear the rat-a-tat of the Exploration Group's machine guns further to the north and would see flares (friendly and enemy) flashing among the shadows down by the lake, while they, always on tenterhooks, watched over their sector. Another night, on 16 December, once again a Ski Company sentry killed a Russian civilian of about 60 years of age. Nobody knew for sure whether he was a partisan or a harmless villager, but there was a move to hold the firer of the shot responsible, which nearly led to a court martial.

As for their equipment, during the first fortnight of December the Company was issued with white hooded capes for camouflage and, for the sentries, a pair of sheepskin overcoats per platoon. In order to protect themselves against the cold, all the volunteers had, off their own bat, equipped themselves with blankets and additional civilian garments such as Russian fur hats. Temperatures were

Podberesje, May 1942, during operations in the Volkhov Pocket. From the left, an unidentified man, Mariano Sánchez-Covisa, another unidentified man, José María Gutiérrez del Castillo (1st Ambulance Platoon), and Virgilio Hernández Rivadulla. The three wearing ponchos, all part of the Ski Company, were operating in the Volkhov Pocket at the time. (José María Gutiérrez del Castillo family collection)

falling to -40 °C and below. Despite these precautions, the weather tested the volunteers' physical resistance as never before, and several men reported sick due to rheumatism, stomach pains, severe colds, etc. An indeterminate number of skis were issued but as there were no ski boots nobody could use them. *General* Moscardó's visit to the Blue Division was cause for celebration since he brought from Spain some special supplies. Each skier received nine cigars, ten packets of cigarettes, and packs of Spanish rolling paper – they had ended up using pages of *"Pravda"* to roll their cigarettes. The rumour also went round that in the New Year, on the 6th to be precise, the Company was going to be relieved and even sent to Riga for rest and relaxation, "where a billet officer is already looking for places for the Spanish to stay". After Christmas the troops received Christmas boxes from the *Führer* and the *Caudillo* with tobacco, coffee, brandy, etc.

The reality turned out to be very different. After spending Christmas Eve in their dugouts and *izbas*, the Ski Company celebrated New Year 1942 among increasingly persistent rumours, not of being relieved, but of an imminent heavy and generalized enemy attack on all sectors of the Volkhov and Lake Ilmen.

The penetration of the German front line in the northern sector of the German 126th Division rang every alarm bell at Blue Division Headquarters. Among other measures it was necessary to tactically reorganize and reinforce the southernmost

The low temperatures rendered the combatants numb with cold. In the photo we see a German soldier turned into a human icicle. (Via authors)

end of the Spanish disposition, defended solely by the Ski Company. After a month of constant duties, the possibility was considered of withdrawing the most battle weary members of the Company from the front line and replacing them with 60 "brave and determined" volunteers from other units. It was also necessary, if at all possible, to increase the unit's firepower and strengthen its command structure.

These were the circumstances when, in the early hours of 8 January 1942, Morozov launched his in-depth attack to the south of Lake Ilmen, which would place the Ski Company at the heart of the decisions that *General* Muñoz Grandes would need to take.

ITEMS OF THE BLUE DIVISION'S EQUIPMENT

- Model 40 helmet from the SE (*Sächsische Emaillier*) factory, batch 859, very probably one of the first issued to the Blue Division at Grafenwöhr.
The year of manufacture is 1941 and it bears the regulation Huber Jordan decal.
- Personalized mess tin found at the Leningrad front.
- Dogtag 182 identifying a member of the 5th Company 263rd Regiment (5th/II/263rd), found in the Novgorod/ Volkhov sector.
- (Private collection via Jaime Sadurní)

4

The Lake Crossing by the Spanish Troops

The Staff of the Blue Division were perfectly aware of both the build-up of Russian forces to the east of Lake Ilmen and their intention to attack Staraya Russa. Therefore once the offensive started, it was no surprise that *General* Von Chappuis, commander of the XXXVIII Army Corps, should call Muñoz Grandes; he lacked reserves to reach Vzvad and liberate it and so asked the Spanish for their help.

The 3rd Staff Section, under the command of *Major* Homar Servera and *General* Muñoz Grandes himself, analysed the possibility of acceding to Chappuis's request. The Blue Division had no reserves with which to carry out the mission. For this reason it fell to the Ski Company to provide support, as the unit closest to Vzvad and tactically ready for such a mission.

While the unit was being alerted and the order given to reinforce it, the operation was studied on the map. The German position was 30 km to the south-east. As the crow flies, the west bank of the lake occupied by the Spanish unit (the village of Spasspiskopez to be precise) and the nearest point on the far side of the lake were separated by just 22.2 km. The fact that the proposed route had already been travelled some weeks earlier by the Exploration Group (a motorized patrol had reached the lighthouse at the mouth of the River Lovat) may well have been taken

Present day view of the south of Lake Ilmen, at Ustreka, the arrival point of the Blue Division Ski Company at the end of their crossing at dawn on 11 January 1942. In the background we see the coast of Sadnoje Pole towards the east. (Via authors)

1. Orthodox Russian cross in memory of the Russians who fell in combat at Ustreka. (José María Manrique)

2. Young Slav woman on the beach at Ustreka, looking out over Lake Ilmen in the direction from where the Spanish troops arrived. (Via authors)

into account. Whatever the case, it was thought to be feasible for the skiers to advance directly to Vzvad in a time of approximately eight hours.

The drums of war began to beat on the west bank of the Ilmen. Muñoz Grandes and *Major* Homar, aboard their sled and protected by an escort, arrived at Babki. They were welcomed and attended to by the new effective commander of the Company, *Captain* Ordás, and by *Lieutenant* Otero de Arce, who stayed on as second in command

The operation was to involve the aforementioned *Captain* Ordás, two sergeants and seven troopers from 3rd Anti-Tank Company; three officers, one sergeant and three soldiers from the Exploration Group; seven carters from the Veterinary Group; twelve soldiers from the 250th Reserve Battalion, plus a pedal-powered radio station manned by men from the Signals Group.

In the early hours of Saturday, 10 January 1942, in the main, indeed only, street of the village of Spasspiskopez, the expeditionary force began to form up. The patrol which had been carrying out a recce by the lake hours earlier was ordered to fall in too, despite having had practically no rest. In total there were a little over 200 men: the skiers (not the entire Company) plus the attached men. A handful of sleds drawn by local horses would be carrying the equipment; nine machine guns (*Maschinengewehr 34*, the legendary MG-34 machine gun) provided for the occasion, ammunition, the radio set, provisions, etc. A number of Russian civilians would also be crossing the lake; one or two as guides and the rest as *panjewagen* (to use the German term), in other words sled drivers. Most of them were the owners of the *troikas* (sleds) and the *panje* (horses) that had been urgently requisitioned for the operation.

Although the Company was equipped with a certain number of skis, leaving aside problems of availability and doubts as to whether the troops actually knew how to use them (the attached troops certainly did not), the operation would be carried out without skis since it was assumed that on the ice of the lake they would be a hindrance rather than a help.

Corvette-Captain Manuel Mora de Figueroa, *General* Muñoz Grandes'

German cemetery at Korostyn, on the southern bank of the Ilmen, two kilometres to the west of Ustreka. (José María Manrique)

adjutant, was there at Spasspiskopez to send off the expedition. He convinced them of the great responsibility they had; the eyes of the German High Command were on them and they could not let down their comrades trapped in Vzvad: "*You will cross the lake. The march will be short but hard. You will face Soviet forces superior in number. If any of you is sick, say so now.*" Nobody spoke up. After ensuring that everything was in order, *Captain* Ordás gave them final instructions and ordered them to leave.

It was mid-morning by the time the expedition set off into the metallic gloom of the lake. The first squad of the Company's 1st Platoon led the formation. Once they had

left solid ground behind them, icy blasts of air started to gust off the surface of the lake. The temperature began to fall alarmingly. Men and horses panted and wheezed as they trod in the prints left in the snow by those in front of them. And despite the felt-lined boots most of them were wearing, and despite the overcoats, capes, caps and breeches covering their bodies and heads, the relentless Arctic cold soon began to take its toll among the volunteers, as did the dreadful solitude of that frozen wilderness from which emanated unnerving sounds of cracking and creaking caused by under-ice currents.

Controlled blasting of the ice of Lake Ilmen carried out by the Spanish troops. (Juan Negreira)

KONSTANTIN GOGUIJONACHVILI
Georgian interpreter

Georgian *Lieutenant* Konstantin Goguijonachvili, cavalry officer of the Tsarist Army and the White Army, serving with the Staff of the Exploration Group, joined the Ski Company to take part in the relief of Vzvad. He was briefly a frostbite casualty although he was soon able to return to active duty.

Born on 29 July 1894, in Batum (Georgia), he fled to Spain after the triumph of the Bolshevik Revolution. During the 1936-1939 Civil War he fought in the Legion and in the Navarre Battalion of the *Requetés* (Carlist militia), losing an eye in action. He joined the Blue Division in July 1941. His knowledge of the language and the country were hugely appreciated by the Spanish military commanders and he served in several different units. His special skills did not prevent him from becoming involved in the actual fighting on many occasions. He saw out the entire campaign until April 1944 when he returned to Spain with the last of the volunteers of the Blue Legion in which he served as head of the Interpretation Service. For his actions during the campaign he was recommended for the Individual Military Medal and was awarded, among other decorations, the War Merit Cross 1st Class with Swords and the Iron Cross 2nd Class. After the war he continued to live in Spain where he worked in the Military History Service as a Russian translator.

An unexpected barrier of ice forced the motley column to interrupt their march. While the 1st Platoon led the column around the obstacle, Ordás authorized the evacuation of the first frostbite casualties to Spasspiskopez. While crossing the barrier, a sled and a horse disappeared into a crevice and were swallowed up by the ice, much to the dismay of the Russian civilians who were surprised by the stubbornness of the Spanish. In the breaks in the ice barrier snow piled up in huge drifts, into which horses sank up to their hocks and soldiers to their waist.

The biting cold did not only affect men and animals but also affected provisions – no blade was able to cut the food –, weapons, and apparatus. In the case of the

CAPTAIN ORDÁS
The best known hero of the Battle of Lake Ilmen

José Manuel Ordás Rodríguez was born in Arriondas, Asturias, on 13 April 1910, the son of Jerónimo Ordás Rodríguez and Carolina Rodríguez Caso. He was living in Oviedo with his parents at the time of the 18 July uprising, whereupon he joined the II Battalion of Infantry Regiment Milán no. 32 as a volunteer, with the rank of non-commissioned sergeant. Until October he took part in the defence of Oviedo

Ordás during the harsh Russian winter 1941/42. (Ordás family collection)

during the siege laid by Popular Front forces. He fought in such exposed positions as Lugones, Alto de Buenavista, the reservoir, and Loma de Pando.

Having been promoted to provisional second lieutenant on 22 January 1937, he fought in Asturias once again, this time with Infantry Regiment Mérida no. 35, IV Battalion, 1st and 2nd Company. In various actions he showed *"impeccable conduct, discipline, great fighting spirit, intelligence, excellent leadership, courage, and devotion to the national cause"*, and was recommended for an Individual Military Medal. He attended promotion courses in Toledo between September and December of 1937, after which he joined Regular Indigenous Forces Group No. 2, IV Tabor (equivalent to a battalion), 1st Company, as a provisional lieutenant. A few weeks after arriving at his new unit he found himself in the thick of the fighting on the Teruel Front where he received a bullet wound in the thigh on 21 December during operations to take Cerro Gordo hill. A month later, on 28 January 1938, he returned to the front, now in the 3rd Company of the same Tabor. During that year he fought with courage and determination at the head of his men in Teruel (Hill 1,188 and Son del Puerto), on the advance towards the Mediterranean (River Mijares, Castellón, Puntal de l'Aljub, and Sierra de Espadán mountains), and on the Ebro Front (Sierra de Pàndols mountains, Hill 353, and Manresa). Unsurprisingly, on 14 August 1939 he was awarded the coveted Individual Military Medal (the first of two).

In the Blue Division, organizing the 3rd Anti-Tank Company in the camp at Grafenwöhr. (Ordás family collection)

Once the Civil War was over, he attended an officer conversion course at the Zaragoza Infantry Academy, at the end of which in July 1941, now a non-commissioned captain, he joined the Blue Division, in which he was given command of the 3rd Anti-Tank Company. On the 24th of the same month he left Grafenwöhr (Germany) for the Russian Front with an expedition made up of a number of officers led by Chief of Staff *Lieutenant-Colonel* Luis Zanón Aldalur. The purpose was to become familiar with the *Wehrmacht*'s combat tactics. They flew, via Berlin, to the Ukranian city of Vinnytsia to the south-west of Kiev. There, between 27 July and 3 September, they were able to take part in the reduction of the Uman pocket. Ordás was attached to the Staff of the 3rd Anti-Tank Company of the 1st Mountain Division. Once reunited with the Blue Division and back at the front, he would deploy his unit on the west bank of Lake Ilmen.

The top brass tasked *Captain* Ordás with the relief of the Vzvad garrison, as recounted in this book. For that operation he was awarded the Individual Military Medal and the Iron Cross 2nd Class. After leave at the rear he returned to the front in the Ilmen sector on 24 March 1942. In April he was awarded the Iron Cross 1st Class, and in May and June, in command of 3rd Anti-Tank Company, he fought in the Volkhov Pocket. He was repatriated in July. He earned the admiration of his superior officers due to his performance in battle and his charismatic character.

In October 1942 he was sent to the Military Household of the Head of State to serve in the Staff and in the Company of Moroccan Riflemen. Promoted to major in July 1949, he was soon sent to the Directorate General of Recruitment and Personnel of the Ministry of the Army in Madrid. His last posting before transitioning to the reserve was as adjutant to *General* Roberto Gómez de Salazar y Orduña.

José Manuel Ordás, whose military bearing earned him the nickname of *The Prussian*, left the army in December 1952 when he was 42 years old for family reasons, to become the Provincial Delegate for Pensions in Cadiz. Two years previously, in 1950, he had married María del Carmen de Aranda y Gutiérrez de Quijano in Jerez de la Frontera. They had four children: three boys and the youngest a girl. According to his family he rarely spoke about his war experiences, and the few times he did, it was because someone had asked him to. He would always return to the same two themes. The first was how the Russian civilian population treated the Spanish; he found

1. Close-up of *Captain* Ordás's Individual Military Medal, with Ilmen and Son del Puerto-Sierra de Espadán ribbon bars. (Regular Army Museum, Ceuta, photo *Second Lieutenant* Pastor)

2. Captain Ordás inside an *izba* with two fellow *divisionarios*. (Ordás family collection)

3. Russia, April 1942. *Major* Homar of the Blue Division Staff, *Lieutenant-Colonel* Sánchez del Águila Menco, commander of the Exploration Group, and *Captain* Ordás at the Iron Cross 2nd Class award ceremony of the second mentioned officer. (Juan Negreira)

them always pleasant and friendly, quite unlike his experience with German officers and soldiers. He never forgot an altercation he had with a German officer which nearly ended with them drawing their pistols. It all started because of the way the German was treating a Russian in his presence. The second abiding memory of his stay in Russia was of the weather. He would never forget the cold. His experience on the Eastern Front marked him forever: he never felt warm again!

He was a deeply religious man. When he was very seriously ill his wife asked her husband's spiritual director how he was prepared for death. She was told not to

Several of the twenty-four decorations awarded to *Captain* Ordás. From left to right: (hanging from the button) Iron Cross 2nd Class. On the medal bar: Red Cross of Military Merit, Defenders of Oviedo Medal 1936-37, Campaign Medal (Civil War), Suffering for the Motherland Medal (wound medal). Behind the latter (almost hidden): Red Cross of Military Merit, White Cross of Military Merit, White Cross of Naval Merit, Cross of San Hermenegildo, Blue Division Volunteers Medal (Spanish Government), Commemorative Medal for Spanish Volunteers in the Struggle Against Bolshevism (Spanish Government) and Winter Campaign in the East Medal 1941-42. Below the medal bar and from left to right: Spanish War Cross, Iron Cross 1st Class, and Anti-Tank Unit badge.

In the centre: Badge of the Order of San Hermenegildo. Below, close to the belt: two Spanish War Crosses. (Regular Army Museum, Ceuta, photo *Second Lieutenant* Pastor)

worry because her husband "was a man of rock-like faith". José Manuel Ordás died in Cadiz, on 8 April 1993.

latter, the first victim was the radio set, which lost its generator and battery to the cold. All communication with the Division had been lost, so *Signals Sergeant* García Ontiveros, with another soldier, had to go back for replacement equipment.

When they came across another ice barrier they had to make another detour. A little later a third barrier reared up together with some impassable crevices, delaying the advance and forcing the column to constantly change direction. The opposite bank was not yet in sight. As a result of the detours, with no reference points in that sea of ice, and compasses rendered useless by the cold, it is no surprise that the expedition veered off course towards the south, but neither *Captain*

Ordás nor the other officers considered going back. And as the night closed in and darkness enveloped them it became obvious to all that they were on the wrong course. They should have reached land hours ago and yet they were still only about halfway across. There was nothing else to do but press on. And the sooner the better. Nobody thought about going back. The last to be evacuated due to frostbite, making a total of twenty-one, should by now have been safely back at Spasspiskopez.

Morale remained admirable, but strength was flagging. Many, feeling unable to walk another step, took refuge in the sleds, unmindful of the danger of not moving in such low temperatures, which increased the risk of frostbite. Doctors and medics tried to help those worst affected by the cold, by massaging their ears and extremities, applying compresses, and distributing sips of vodka. It was, however, necessary to administer this typical cold-resistant Russian drink with precaution since below -50 °C all its ingredients except for the alcohol would freeze.

1. Men of the Ski Company, one of them with skis, which were not used on the lake crossing. (Guillermo González de Canales)

2. *Cavalry Lieutenant* Bernardino Domínguez Díaz-Maza of the 2nd Squadron of the Exploration Group was attached to the Ski Company and fought at Lake Ilmen, emerging unscathed from the battle. (Via authors)

3. Francisco García Ontiveros skiing on the Russian Front. Although he took part in the Lake Ilmen operation, he did not actually belong to the Ski Company. (García Ontiveros family collection)

SERGEANT FRANCISCO GARCÍA ONTIVEROS
One of the heroes of Signals in the battle of the Ilmen

Francisco García Ontiveros was born in Luque, Cordoba, on 1 September 1919. He fought in the Civil War from 1 May 1937 as a radio operator on the side of the Nationalists. While serving in the Air Signals Regiment with the rank of provisional sergeant he joined the Blue Division, in which he served in the 2nd Platoon of the Radio Company of the Signals Group.

At the front he distinguished himself in the River Volkhov crossing operations on 20 October 1941 in which he *"constantly maintained the communications he was in charge of and showed at all times technical capacity and leadership skills"*, according to a report written by the lieutenant leading his platoon. In subsequent fighting at the Otenski and Possad bridgeheads he performed equally well. Despite intense artillery fire and continuous Soviet counterattacks, the squad under the command of García Ontiveros, in which *Sergeant* Rafael Foronda Zudaire also served, managed to keep open the lines of communications in their charge. Their radio station was Kl.a1, comprising the two aforementioned officers, drivers Calixto Álvaro Ribas and José Luis León Sancho, corporals Martín Díaz Garcés and Vicente Montero Moreno, and troopers Francisco Garrido Jiménez and Casiano Santamaría Boto. The group's high level of technical skills, great courage and spirit of service – its components fought alongside the infantry in defence of its positions – earned it the recognition of its superiors, as did their initiative, reliability and the speed with which they repaired any faults. On 16 November the company's captain, Carlos Haurie González, personally congratulated Francisco for having carried out a magnificent radio watchkeeping service.

On his return to Grigorovo, he was sent to Staraya Rakoma, on Lake Ilmen, to serve with the Exploration Group. On 21 November 1941, having just arrived, he took part in his first operation, establishing a radio link with a platoon of the Exploration Group, which was reporting to HQ on the state of the lake. From 15.15 h his station was operating out of Nawinki alongside another German station, maintaining a constant link with Headquarters throughout the night. This action led the radio company's captain to propose *Sergeant* García Ontiveros and *Private* Manuel Escobedo Telena for official recognition *"of their diligent service, showing excellent military spirit, iron discipline, and great devotion to the service."*

When the mission to rescue the Vzvad garrison was planned, García Ontiveros's radio station was the one chosen to go with the Skiers.

Meanwhile, by following the tracks made by the column, *Sergeant* García Ontiveros had rejoined the unit with a new generator, thereby re-establishing communication with the Division. The Blue Division's operations journal keeps a record of the radio messages between headquarters and the Ski Company.

Muñoz Grandes passed on information from Von Chappuis and tried to give encouragement to Ordás and his men. At 21.30 h on the 10th he told them: *"The Vzvad garrison is resisting courageously. It must be saved, for the honour of Spain and the spirit of brotherhood between our two nations (…). Keep your spirits up; you have glory within your grasp. Attack with decision."* At 00.02 h on the 11th there was a new message: *"I know how much you are suffering. That's not what matters. The whole of Spain will know about your feat. Germany admires you. You are the pride of our race. I have faith in you because I have faith in Spain. Trust in God and attack like Spaniards."*

These epic dispatches demonstrate two things; the legendary nature of the operation as it was seen by the Blue Division commanders, and also a certain degree of blindness on their part. Muñoz Grandes and his General Staff thought Ordás was just a short distance from the bank and about to enter into combat. Nothing was further from the truth, a truth that is much better recounted by two of the men who took part in the crossing, both members of the Ski Company, Ángel Aybar Redondo of the Staff and Alberto Coscolla Teixidor of the 1st Platoon. The former commented, *"The biggest operation I was involved in was the famous Lake Ilmen crossing. I was one of the few who managed to escape frostbite and emerge unscathed from the fighting. I protected my feet from the cold, something which affected many of my fellow soldiers, very well because from the start I wore a pair of* valenki, *felt-lined Russian boots. The cold on the lake was something hard for anyone not there to imagine; I don't think our commanders realized what we were actually doing until it was all over. Not even the local inhabitants dared to cross it in mid-winter. Some people have said that the Ilmen affair was not such a big deal; that it was cold on the whole of the front and that the feat was blown up for propaganda purposes. I would have liked to see them with me, at 50 below zero on the frozen surface of the middle of the lake and with a blizzard blowing. It was unbearable; if we'd known what was in store for us on the lake I think we'd have mutinied before setting out, because they were sending us out to be frozen to death. But we had to save the Germans; we had to do it for them and for Spain. After some unforgettable words of encouragement we set out on our adventure.*

"I was at the head of the column with Lieutenant Otero de Arce, who was *second-in-command now since our commander was another officer,* Captain Ordás, *and I soon began to realize the intensity of the cold, which would do for [so many of] us. Casualties were being sent to the rear but we had to press on. After the crossing, over half of the 200 men who set out were casualties."*

In his memoirs Alberto Coscolla Teixidor describes the last hours of that apocalyptic march:

> *"The immense cold became even worse and the men looked like marching blocks of ice. Even the dark coats of the Siberian horses were whitened with frost, making the animals pulling sleds look as if they had aged 100 years in just a few hours. Some soldiers were complaining, screaming wildly 'my feet! my feet!' as they thrashed on the ground like animals struck by lightning. Others beat their chests savagely to get some life back in their bodies, until the cold mercifully anaesthetized their terrible pain."*

They came across a hole in the ice made by fishermen, which told them that land could not be so very far away.

But it was two hours later when, at the bleak white dawn of 11 January 1942, the vanguard of the Ski Company spotted the shore and the outline of a village. The 1st Platoon, with *Lieutenant* Castañer in the centre and *Sergeant* Montaña to the left, deployed on the ice in battle order. Two flares crossed the misty sky. One of the men (some sources say Alberto Coscolla Teixidor and others Mariano Sánchez Covisa) went forward to see what troops were presumably manning the village.

SOVIET RIFLEMAN'S EQUIPMENT, 1941-1942
(COLLECTION OF MANUEL PÉREZ RUBIO)

- The legendary PPSh-41 sub-machine gun, nicknamed *"naranjero"* (the name in Spanish given to any big bore gun, presumably because they were big enough to fire oranges), with a magazine and magazine holder. This versatile weapon started to be issued to Soviet units as from November 1941.
- Also shown is a 1938 banknote and three original medals of the Second World War. The one on the right is the highest Russian decoration: the Order of the Red Flag. Created in 1918 at the time of the Revolution, the model current in 1941 had a ribbon attached. The one in the middle is the "Order of the Red Star" and to the left, the medal "For Services in Battle" with the old ribbon system.

A small Spanish column on the vastness of Lake Ilmen, advancing over its frozen surface.
(Juan Negreira).

It was with great relief that he ascertained that they were Germans of the 290th
Division. But relief turned into concern when they also discovered that the village
in question, Ustreka, was a long way from their objective; they had marched for
twenty-two hours to end up so far from Vzvad! Lake Ilmen had taken a terrible
toll on those who had dared to cross it. For the rest of the day *Lieutenant* Sánchez
Bejarano and *Sergeant* Cifuentes, aided by medics from the German detachment
and civilians from Ustreka, did everything they could to attend to the skiers. The
effort and the cold had caused most of the men to be suffering from extreme
exhaustion and frostbite. A fair number could be returned to service thanks to
the work efforts of those manning the first aid station, but many lost their ears,
fingers, toes, feet, or nose to frostbite. The ice had reduced the force's strength by
over a half; there were 102 casualties, 46 of which were evacuated that same day
and the other 56 the following day. All were sent to hospitals of the 16th Army
situated to the west of Lake Ilmen, at Medved, Soltsy, and Dno.

RADIO DISPATCH ON 11 JANUARY 1942

*"10:30 hours. General Muñoz Grandes to Captain Ordás. I know what you had to endure
during the arduous march you have completed. If good fortune was not with us and your
mission is not a total success you are not to blame. The Vzvad garrison is still holding on
valiantly and we need to go to its aid whatever the cost, even if all our men perish out
there on the ice, even if only a few survive, even just you. Press on to the death. Everything
for the heroism of the defenders of Vzvad. Either we save them or we die with them. On
behalf of our country, I thank you. And do not falter. I have faith in you. Muñoz Grandes."*

MARIANO SÁNCHEZ-COVISA CARRO
Seasoned fighter and political activist

The son of Mariano Sánchez-Covisa Rivero and María Visitación Carro, he was born in Madrid on 15 April 1919 (he had four siblings). In the Civil War he was first jailed and then recruited by the People's Army in which he served for seven months on the Madrid Front with the 1st Company of Sappers of the 1st Division. He was studying chemistry and was head of the mountain section of the National Sports Delegation of the SEU when he signed up for the Blue Division. Shortly after the unit reached the front he showed his fighting spirit as an ambulance driver at the Volkhov Bridgehead. In October and November 1941, with his inseparable friend Hernández Rivadulla, he found himself in highly dangerous situations, often under enemy fire. A born athlete, he asked to transfer to the Skiers Company in time to take part in the Battle of Lake Ilmen. He was one of the many casualties; on 24 January 1942 he was evacuated with first degree frostbite in his right hand. He was discharged from the hospital at Charlottenburg on 17 March and was able to return to the front to continue fighting until his repatriation. Among other decorations he received the Infantry Assault Badge.

Back from the Russian campaign he became a lifelong active member of the Falangist movement. He was imprisoned in the aftermath of the alleged assassination attempt on *General* Varela, a murky event that took place at the shrine of the Virgin of Begoña in August 1942. It would not be the only time in his life he was arrested. During Spain's political transition he became involved in various projects, particularly in the organization *"Guerrilleros de Cristo Rey"* (Warriors of Christ the King) which he founded with a group of like-minded people. He was a man at odds with convention; he was not afraid to take his ideas to the street, where he took part in demonstrations (some violent), brawls, poster sticking, etc. He never married. He was a sincere, passionate Catholic and ultramontanist who died of a heart attack while walking the Way of St James with a group of friends on 24 September 1993.

5

Containment Engagements to the South of Lake Ilmen and Evacuation of Vzvad

As we saw in Chapter 2, on 11 January 1942 the epicentre of the entire German sector to the south of Lake Ilmen was the encircled town of Staraya Russa. While Erdmannsdorff fought tooth and nail to defend this town, hoping for the imminent arrival of the promised reinforcements, Hansen tried to contain the enemy advance on his northern flank, using for this purpose *Captain* Ordás's men. It was vital to prevent the Russians from advancing along the south-south-west shore of the lake and penetrating as far as Shimsk, as this would endanger the entire 16th Army.

With their base at Ustreka and in the state they were in, the remnants of the Ski Company could not be expected to undertake the mission entrusted to them on their own. They were in a sector defended by Germans and a long way from Vzvad, some 11-12 km as the crow flies. This was an unthinkable distance under

Divisionarios on the banks of Lake Ilmen. (Quintana Lacaci family collection)

A village in the Ski Company's area of operations. (Authors' collection)

the current circumstances, not only because the terrain offered little in the way of roads but also because it was crawling with enemy troops.

In this dramatic scenario events were unfolding rapidly, driven by the operations to defend Staraya Russa. The priority for the 16th Army was to save this point; the relief of Vzvad was a secondary, not to say unattainable, objective. Muñoz Grandes assumed that his skiers, while they would remain under his command, would ultimately be under the orders of *General* Hansen, commander of the X Army Corps, and more directly, *Captain* Lüer of the 290th Division, in charge of the battle group which was delighted to have the Spanish troops join them in such an unexpected manner. Therefore from that moment on, for tactical purposes the Ski Company would receive orders from *Kampfgruppe* commander Lüer, whose headquarters was at Borisovo. However, Ordás continued to send reports over the radio to Muñoz Grandes who, in turn, remained in open communication with Chappuis and Busch.

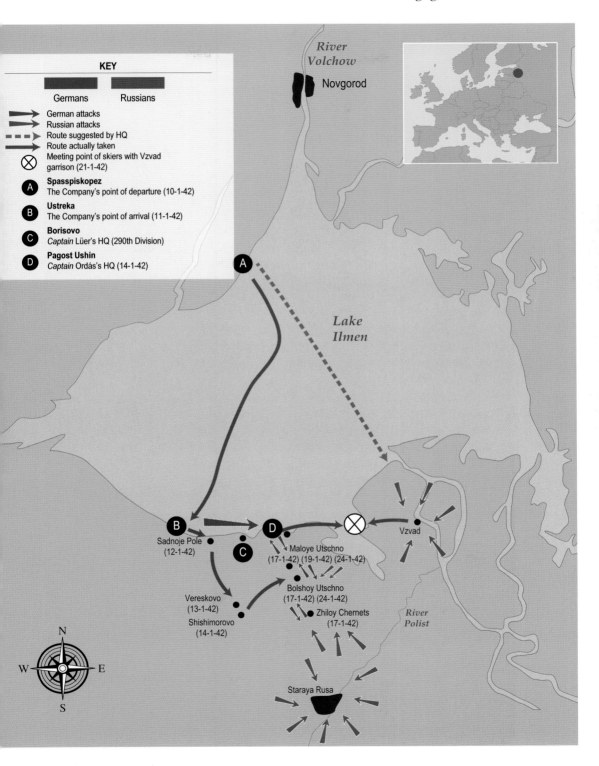

KEY

Germans	Russians

German attacks
Russian attacks
Route suggested by HQ
Route actually taken

⊗ Meeting point of skiers with Vzvad garrison (21-1-42)

A **Spasspiskopez**
The Company's point of departure (10-1-42)

B **Ustreka**
The Company's point of arrival (11-1-42)

C **Borisovo**
Captain Lüer's HQ (290th Division)

D **Pagost Ushin**
Captain Ordás's HQ (14-1-42)

River Volchow

Novgorod

Lake Ilmen

A

B
Sadnoje Pole
(12-1-42)

C

D

Maloye Utschno
(17-1-42) (19-1-42) (24-1-42)

⊗

Vzvad

Vereskovo
(13-1-42)

Shishimorovo
(14-1-42)

Bolshoy Utschno
(17-1-42) (24-1-42)

Zhiloy Chernets
(17-1-42)

River Polist

Staraya Rusa

N
W   E
S

ÁNGEL ALONSO HERNÁNDEZ
Corporal of the Ski Company

Ángel Alonso Hernández was born on 1 March 1924 in Chillarón del Rey (Guadalajara) into a family of traders. Besides Ángel, the first born, his parents, Paulino and Margarita, had two daughters.

When Ángel was still a child, the family moved to Madrid and spent the Civil War there. In 1939 Ángel joined the Falangist movement, forming part of the *Centuria* (equivalent to a company) "*Leones de Castilla*", to which other *divisionario*s also belonged, such as Santiago Hernández Ramos (who served in the 5th/269) and Fernando de Jesús, who after the Russian campaign would become a lay Jesuit. And like Santiago, Ángel, a staunch Falangist, jumped at the chance to join the Blue Division, which he did without parental permission after lying about his age (the latter was not a problem as the lad was a towering 6 foot 3).

As a Corporal in the Ski Company's staff, he survived the Vzvad rescue operation without so much as a scratch. But it was not easy for him to assimilate everything he had experienced and suffered. Ángel was not a man who liked to talk about his time with the Blue Division, but the few times he did, the picture he painted was one of a life or death struggle for survival in a hostile environment, facing an enemy that was prepared to fight to the death.

Four months after Lake Ilmen, on 20 May 1942, he returned to Spain to enjoy a twenty-nine-day leave. But Ángel, by nature a creative and restless young man, used the time to apply for authorization from the Directorate General of Civil Aviation to attend a glider pilot course at the Huesca training school in

1. Iron Cross 2nd Class awarded to Ángel Alonso for his participation in the Battle of Lake Ilmen.

2. Infantry Assault Badge awarded to *divisionario* Ángel Alonso.

3. Badge identifying the wearer as a qualified glider pilot (Grade C). Ángel Alonso obtained his at Huesca in 1942. (Private collection)

4. The Falangist *centuria* of Ángel Alonso (marked with a white square) was invited to a meeting in Rome, together with other youth organizations from Germany and Hungary. The photo captures the moment when they marched past Ettore Muti, the secretary of the Italian Fascist party.

5. Ángel at the controls of a Schneider Grunau Baby glider during his time at Huesca. (All images from Alonso family archive)

order to obtain his Grade C licence as a glider pilot (in 1941 he had already obtained his Grade B licence). This prevented him from returning to Russia, although in official documentation he is listed as having been repatriated on 9 December 1942. The fact is that in November of that year he was still in Huesca attending the course (which had started on 1 July). His parents took advantage of the situation to ask the authorities not allow him to return to the Blue Division since he was still under age.

After a number of years which he basically spent travelling and enjoying his youth, Ángel decided it was time to settle down. As a lover of mountains and skiing, in the early 1950s he set up a skiing business, first in Navacerrada in the mountains north of Madrid and later also in Madrid itself. In 1957 he married María Teresa, a girl from Seville whom he met while she was spending the summer in Navacerrada, and they had five children.

Ángel remained in close contact and on friendly terms with his fellow Blue Division veterans, especially Arturo de Gregorio. Those who knew him described him as a man who was easy going and fun to be with, and who treated other people with courtesy and respect. He was a loving husband and father and a good friend to his friends, among whom was Father Ángel García, the founder of the NGO "Messengers of Peace".

He died in Madrid, on 10 December 1977. The cause was a virus which affected his brain and took less than a month to kill him.

With no time to rest, in the early hours of 12 January what was left of the Ski Company, just over seventy men, moved to nearby Sadnoje Pole on the banks of Lake Ilmen to reinforce its garrison, which was made up of ninety second-line German troops.

On the following day three patrols ventured from Sadnoje Pole; two of them with twelve men each struck out towards Pagost Ushin and the coast of the lake, and the third, with twenty-two men, headed for Staraya Russa. This latter group intended to reconnoitre the route to Vereskovo, a small village five kilometres to the south, which by that night they would be occupying, along with a group of thirty Germans.

On 14 January Pagost Ushin and Shishimorovo were occupied. The first operation was carried out by *Lieutenant* Castañer, leading a force of two officers and thirty-two soldiers, while the second was led by *Lieutenant* Otero de Arce with twelve men out of Vereskovo who drove off an enemy patrol. At the end of that day the Spanish skiers were reinforced by fresh troops, Germans of the 174th Regiment (81st Division) and Latvians of the 16th Auxiliary Police Battalion, who had recently arrived in the sector. At both Pagost Ushin and Shishimorovo their respective garrisons repulsed a number of attacks and took several prisoners. These prisoners were duly interrogated and revealed that there were around "3,000 skiers", a figure which the authors find hard to believe (if it refers to the particular sector in which the Spanish were operating), but nevertheless gives an indication of the large number of enemy troops active in the area.

After an exchange of views with *Captain* Lüer, and acting against the orders of his superiors who on the 16th told him to return to the Blue Division, *Captain*

Borisovo, home to the command post of *Captain* Lüer of the 290th Infantry Division. (AHSR)

Izba near Ustreka. (Authors' collection)

Ordás held his position in the fishing village of Pagost Ushin. For Ordás it was a matter of honour to complete the mission he had been entrusted with. He refused to relinquish the position it had taken his force such a huge effort to reach, preferring to remain there ready, if required, to go to the aid of the Vzvad garrison, break the siege, and then withdraw to the rear.

On 15 January a truck sent from the Blue Division with supplies of warm clothing and some skis for the Company had managed to reach Sadnoje Pole. A number of frostbite casualties were sent back in the truck, among them Guillermo González de Canales who preferred to go to the Spanish hospital at Grigorowo rather than a German one (shortly afterwards he would be evacuated to Riga). By then Virgilio Hernández Rivadulla and Jorge Hernández Bravo, two Company volunteers, had already rejoined the unit. On their way to Riga, where they had been sent to acquire equipment for the unit, they turned around when they found out about the operation undertaken by their fellow soldiers. Another man to reappear was Julián Martín Fabiani who, like the others, arrived by motorized transport skirting around the lake. Another three riflemen ready for battle, who were not exhausted from having crossed the lake, were a most valuable addition to the Spanish force.

Given that the enemy was on the verge of capturing Staraya Russa, which would have been catastrophic for German interests, Vzvad had lost all strategic importance. Therefore our skiers were not sent eastwards, in the direction of Vzvad, but instead were sent south, towards Staraya Russa. At that moment it was imperative to neutralize the threat posed by a number of villages to the south of Pagost Ushin, already in Russian hands.

Russian orthodox church near Pagost Ushin. (AHSR)

VIRGILIO HERNÁNDEZ RIVADULLA
A man of legend

The charismatic and multifaceted Virgilio Hernández Rivadulla is, at the time of writing (2016), the only surviving Blue Division veteran of the Ski Company that we know about. Born in Madrid, on 28 April 1921, during the Spanish Civil War he was sent by his family to Barcelona where he worked as a waiter and qualified as a medical practitioner. He was mobilized in 1938 and served as a *Second Lieutenant (medical)* in an anti-aircraft unit of the People's Army, the 538th Battery of the DECA (Special Defence Against Aircraft) to be precise. In January 1939 the battery provided anti-aircraft protection for the last Cabinet meeting of the Republican Government. He fled to France, where he was interned in the Argelés concentration camp. After a bad experience with

Communists, he swore to fight Communism wherever he could. He was able to return to Spain, where he spent some time in two POW camps. Once free he started to study journalism and also became involved in various sports (which would go on to play an important role throughout his civilian life).

Virgilio left for the Russian Front in July 1941. Although he initially served with the 1st Ambulance Platoon, his thirst for action and his ability to ski led him to join the recently formed Ski Company, along with his friend *Lieutenant* Castañer Enseñat who, in Virgilio's own words *"had never seen a ski in his life"*. He did not take part in the epic Lake Ilmen crossing, but rejoined the Ski Company just in time to fight in the freezing conditions south of the lake. He was evacuated with frostbite, but on being discharged he returned to the front in April 1942, where he was involved in the fighting in the Volkhov Pocket. He was repatriated to Spain in August the same year, in time to be implicated in the Basilica of Begoña bomb incident in Bilbao, for which he was tried and sentenced. On his release from prison in late 1943, he studied and graduated in law and journalism. He went on to have a successful career in sports journalism, specializing in the field of motorsport. He worked for the daily sports newspaper *MARCA*, for the magazine *MOTOCICLISMO*, and on RTVE, the Spanish national broadcasting network. He was married to Irene Urraburu Bueno with whom he had four children.

On 17 January the remains of the Ski Company together with a group of forty Latvians embarked on an operation that culminated in a particularly hard-fought battle. *Captain* Ordás directed the attack from his command post at Pagost Ushin. The Spanish column, comprising thirty-six men under the command of *Lieutenant* Otero de Arce, was split into three small platoons under the respective command of *lieutenants* Castañer, Velasco del Val, and García Porta.

The march, although arduous due to the huge amount of snow on the ground, was largely uneventful until mid-morning. While Maloye Utschno and Bolshoy Utschno were captured without opposition, not so the village of Zhiloy Chernets, further to the south and nestling between dense woods. Here the Russians offered strong resistance inflicting several casualties, but the Spanish skiers, brandishing their rifles and throwing hand grenades, entered the village and overran all enemy strong points. Such was their impetus that the two patrols pursued the Russians well south of the village.

However, the enemy rallied and counterattacked with a strong force and five tanks. The pressure on Zhiloy Chernets was soon irresistible and the right flank quickly gave way, compromising the rest of the unit. The lack of anti-tank weapons made withdrawal to Bolshoy Utschno inevitable, leaving behind several dead and wounded. In this village, however, the Spanish and Latvians were able to keep the enemy infantry at bay with an effective barrage of rifle and machine-gun fire, preventing the supporting tanks from advancing. Instead they fired incendiary shells into the village from range, setting a number of *izbas* ablaze. The situation became unsustainable and the defenders, decimated by Russian

1. German troops advancing behind a Panzer. (Authors' collection)

2. A fearsome enemy for Germans and Spanish alike; Russian snipers, crack shots and masters of camouflage. (Authors' collection)

automatic weapon fire, held on until 15.00h when they were given the order to fall back to Maloye Utschno where, with the aid of an anti-tank gun provided by a German platoon, they were able to organize a more substantial defence. The day's casualties were terrible: fifteen dead and thirteen wounded.

The *divisionario* O.S. tells of the nightmarish retreat to Maloye Utschno and Pagost Ushin:

"*The Russians attacked the village with tanks. I was in one of the first houses, standing up and firing. One of my fellow soldiers – Manuel Herrero – told me to kneel down because they were going to hit me; the Russians were only a short distance away from us. I paid no attention to him and carried on firing from a standing position. I was hit in the thigh (if I'd been kneeling down I'd have been shot in the head!). I was taken with other wounded men to an abandoned house. On the short journey all I could see were dead bodies all over the place. Once inside the house that was serving as a first aid post I saw how bullets were passing through the walls. There were another 30 wounded soldiers lying on the ground. We started to hear the noise of the engines of the Russian tanks out in the street. Suddenly the door opened and Virgilio appeared, picking me up and getting me out of there however he could. 'Come on, down here!' he said. I was the only one to get out of there... The others shouted for Virgilio to get them out, but he couldn't. The Russians killed them. He saved my life. Down the street were Jorge Hernández and a sergeant and they evacuated me. Virgilio quickly grabbed a mattress from an old woman's house. They put me on a* troika *with some other wounded men. It was driven by a Latvian. We went along the road which the Russians were heading for as well and I remember that the Latvian leapt off the* troika *while it was still moving and started firing at them. The horse covered the five kilometres between the village and the aid post without a driver (my mother always said that it was a miracle of the Virgin). The man who was lying next to me, on the side the Russians were shooting at, was dead when we arrived. I suppose the Latvian driver was killed too, because the Russians were almost on top of us... We could see them!*"

A Soviet sapper standing by a car. (Authors' collection)

ÁNGEL AYBAR REDONDO
The youngest member of the Ski Company

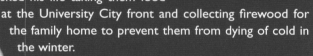

Ángel Aybar Redondo was born in Madrid on 18 July 1926, the son of the multi-talented Saturnino Aybar Notario (a variety performer and print manager on the *ABC* newspaper, among other things) and Antonia Redondo Vázquez. There were five siblings: Antonio, Saturnino, Rosario, Ángel and Pilar. His father and his two elder brothers were mobilized by the Republic during the defence of Madrid, and Ángel risked his life taking them food at the University City front and collecting firewood for the family home to prevent them from dying of cold in the winter.

While only 15 years old and a member of the *Centuria de Montañeros del Frente de Juventudes* (Mountain Company of the Youth Front), he joined the Blue Division. Ángel requested a transfer from the 2nd Radio Company to the Skiers Company. He survived the Battle of Lake Ilmen and was awarded, among other medals, the Iron Cross 2nd Class, the Infantry Assault Badge, and the Collective Military Medal. Back in Spain he had to complete his compulsory military service, which he served in the IPS (*Instrucción Preliminar Superior*). In civilian life, as a graduate from the ICAI School of Engineering he worked at Madrid City Council until his retirement. When Tierno Galván became the new Mayor, Ángel went to see him to complain about how he was being treated by his leftist colleagues, saying *"they are always getting at me for having been in Russia"*. Tierno told him not to worry. They never bothered him again. He spent long periods of time in Santiago de la Ribera (Murcia), where his sister Pilar and his nephews and nieces would join him for holidays. Plagued by stomach ulcers, he was a religious man, an avid reader and a chess player. He died still single in Madrid on 3 May 2010.

With the enemy advance momentarily at a halt, the 18th was a day of rest and respite for the unit. However, the depleted unit was to prove incapable of defending Maloye Utschno from the mass attack launched by the enemy at 07.00 h the following day, under cover of a heavy blizzard that reduced visibility to almost zero.

The laconic but graphic dispatch sent by *Captain* Ordás to *General* Muñoz Grandes, late on 19 January 1942, provides the best summary of the bloodiest battle fought by the Ski Company and their German comrades:

> "*At seven hundred hours today the enemy entered Maloye Utschno in massive numbers, attacking our garrison consisting of twenty-three Spaniards and nineteen Germans. Attack supported by six tanks. Rest of Company deployed; five Spanish and two German wounded brought in. Huge enemy superiority supported by tanks prevent us from retaking position. The garrison has not surrendered; it is going down fighting. We see a large enemy concentration at Maloye Utschno and Bolshoy Utschno. We expect attack. We will know how to die like Spaniards.* Arriba Spain. Viva Franco."

In the end the expertise of Otero de Arce's patrol, which at the end of the day was able to reach the outskirts of Maloye Utschno, made it possible to save seven of the wounded from certain death from frostbite. The balance for the day, 35 casualties between dead and wounded, was devastating. The Spanish Ski Company had been wiped out as a combat unit.

We shall leave the little over thirty Spanish men defending Pagost Ushin from the aerial bombing and attacks by the enemy infantry, and move eastwards, towards Vzvad. Once the situation at Staraya Russa had been stabilized, it made no sense

A German infantryman, in this case well protected against the low temperatures, scanning the front. (Via authors)

Three Spanish riflemen, dressed in white, pose for the camera of the *Propaganda-Kompanie der Armee Busch* (Propaganda Company of the Busch's 16th Army). (Via authors)

for the OKW to continue holding onto Vzvad when there were no longer enough men available to think about retaking the surrounding area. For this reason, Pröhl, as we mentioned earlier, continued to be authorized to withdraw whenever he thought it appropriate.

As late as the night of 19 January, the same day the Spanish Ski Company were being slaughtered in Maloye Utschno, Vzvad withstood a similar mass attack. Russian infantry and several tanks managed to break into the town, reaching nearly as far as the sauna and the collective farm store. The fighting was at very close quarters, hand-to-hand between the men, while as many as four Russian tanks were destroyed with hand grenades and Molotov cocktails. German casualties were high; seventeen dead and dozens of wounded. It no longer made any sense to hold Vzvad.

Throughout the following day preparations were made for a withdrawal. Nothing of any use to the enemy was to be left behind. Whatever could not be carried away had to be destroyed. The heavy guns and the "Freya" radar were destroyed, the latter blown up by the man in charge of it, *Lieutenant* Schneider of the 6th Company of the 1st Signals Regiment of the *Luftwaffe*. The last unburied dead were laid to rest in a mass grave dug with the aid of explosives.

When night fell on the following day the evacuation began. While three squads fired on the Russian lines, the bulk of the garrison, including the Russian collaborators, headed westwards across the frozen marshland towards Tuleblskiy Bay on Lake Ilmen. The journey was slow and arduous, not only because of the intense cold (temperatures continued to be appalling but had actually risen to -35 °C), but due to the depth of the snow and the threat from Russian patrols which harassed the three defending squads which had succeeded in rejoining the column.

The Ski Company had been warned of the movement that the Vzvad garrison was about to make. A seven man patrol under the command of *Lieutenant* Otero de Arce set out from Pagost Ushin in the early hours of the morning to cover the withdrawal, pushing east out onto the lake. When the two forces spotted each other in the darkness, they launched the agreed sequence and colour of flares and, before dawn on 21 January, the Spanish at last met the German vanguard in the middle of the lake, at a point almost equidistant between Pagost Ushin and Vzvad.

TOMÁS ARCHELY
Wounded at Lake Ilmen

Tomás Archely Fernández was born in Valladolid in the district of San Juan into a large, working class family. In the Second Republic he and his brother Ignacio took part in the activities of the *Pioneros Socialistas* youth group. When the Civil War broke out, Ignacio was captured and imprisoned in Fort San Cristóbal (Pamplona) while Tomás joined the Falangists with whom he served in an automotive unit. He joined the first contingent of the Blue Division in Valladolid, where he transferred from the Anti-Tank Group to the Ski Company. At the Battle of Lake Ilmen he was wounded in action. He was repatriated in May 1942 having been awarded a Spanish War Cross and a Red Cross of Military Merit, among other medals. Another younger brother, Jesús, joined up later and served in the 5th Company of the 262nd Regiment. In civilian life Tomás worked at SAVA, a vehicle manufacturer based in Valladolid. Independent and adventurous, he married Cisteta, a widow, but had no children. Tomás was not known to have any friends. The date of his death is unknown.

The meeting was memorable; Otero de Arce and Pröhl joined in an emotional hug. Together and at the greatest possible speed, since the lives of the wounded were at stake due to the low temperatures, they covered the few kilometres that separated them from Pagost Ushin. As his exhausted Germans finally reached Pagost Ushin, *Captain* Pröhl paid his respects to *Captain* Ordás, who accommodated the newly arrived troops and organized the urgent evacuation of the wounded to Borisovo where Lüer had set up an aid post.

High Command wanted to prop up the northernmost end of the X Army Corps abutting Lake Ilmen, so two days later a column of the 174th Regiment arrived at Pagost Ushin. With part of these reinforcements, on 24 January a new operation would be set in motion, involving the remaining survivors of the Ski Company.

Two German platoons and one Spanish platoon, under the command of *lieutenants* Otero de Arce and Castañer, set off at 07.00 h supported by two *Panzer* IV tanks in the vanguard. The temperature had dropped to -50 °C, rendering sub-machine guns and rifles unusable. At Maloye Utschno the men had to use machine pistols and hand grenades, but finally they dislodged the defenders, killing a large number of them and capturing prisoners and war materiel. The Blue

1. A graphic Soviet postcard. (Via authors)

2. A Blue Division patrol, wearing winter camouflage and armed to the teeth. In the background, Lake Ilmen (Propaganda Company of the 16th Army). (Via authors)

3. A Blue Division sled passing through a Russian village. (Juan Negreira)

Division skiers saw the bodies of several of their fellow soldiers killed five days previously, both Spanish and Latvians. Among the dead were *Second Lieutenant* García Larios and *Interpreter Sergeant* Miguel Schumacher.

The column continued on to Bolshoy Utschno where Russian resistance was much stiffer due to a tank positioned at the entrance to the village. Until the 7.5 cm shells of the German *Panzers* knocked it out, the column was unable to enter. When it did, it made short work of clearing out the last of the Russian defenders. At the end of the day, the eight casualties of the Spanish Ski Company (six wounded and two frostbite victims) were evacuated to Pagost Ushin. *Lieutenant* Otero and his remaining soldiers would stay at Bolshoy Utschno, under continuous air bombardment, for two more days. In the morning of 27 January they received orders to fall back to Maloye Utschno and from there to Pagost Ushino.

By then the Ski Company was scarcely a shadow of its former self. On 28 January the dozen uninjured survivors of the unit were ordered to withdraw to the rear at Sadnoje Pole. One of the last casualties was *Lieutenant* Otero de Arce; the officer who had taken part in every battle, who had been respected by bullets and shrapnel alike, finally fell victim of frostbite of the face and ears. Relieved of duties, he was sent to the rear to receive hospital treatment.

MIGUEL PIERNAVIEJA DEL POZO
Falangist "Old Shirt", *divisionario*, journalist, and Lake Ilmen casualty

Before joining the Blue Division, Miguel Piernavieja del Pozo was already a Falangist of some note. Having escaped from Republican held Madrid during the war, he belonged to the National Sports Delegation (he was an Olympic swimmer in 1936) and was an activist for the Falangist Youth Front and Foreign Service. In fact, until just before joining the Blue Division, he had worked for a short time at the Spanish Embassy in London.

Miguel transferred from the Medical Group to the Ski Company, taking part in several patrols before crossing Lake Ilmen and fighting at Maloye Utschno. There, on 17 January 1942, he received a bullet wound in the chest. He underwent a life or death operation at the field hospital at Borisovo before being evacuated to Riga where he was the subject of many anecdotes due to his extrovert nature and physical fortitude. His right lung was damaged but that did not prevent him from smoking; he was even known to blow out the smoke through his open chest wound. Once recovered, he remained in Riga where he married Dzidra Rozitis, daughter of the famous writer Pavils Rozitis, considered a national treasure in Latvia. In 1944, the couple set up home in Spain, where Piernavieja worked in sports journalism and at the Ministry of Information and Tourism as a censor. He had two children and died on 8 June 1983 in Madrid at the age of 67.

1. In the photo, taken at Riga during 1943, we see, from left to right, an unknown person, *Pharmaceutical Captain* Nicolás Zamanillo y González del Camino, brother of the famous José Luis Zamanillo, who was National Delegate of the *Requetés* (the Carlist militia) before the war, as well as holding many other political positions, a German nurse, Piernavieja, and *Pharmaceutical Corporal* Francisco de Miguel González. (Elsa de Miguel Grigans)

2. Blue Division shield with the Falangist yoke and arrows. (Private collection)

3. Badge of the Falangist Foreign Service. (Luis Miguel Sánchez Pérez)

Spanish skier on Lake Ilmen, ready to fire (Propaganda Company of the 16th Army). (Via authors)

On 6 February 1942, what was left of the Ski Company left Sadnoje Pole to rejoin the Blue Division. They left behind thirty-two fellow soldiers, either dead or missing in action. On the 8th of the month the survivors arrived at Grigorowo where they were greeted as authentic heroes. While *Lieutenant* Castañer remained on the Ilmen front in charge of the Company's depot and the few men who had not taken part in the operation, *Captain* Ordás, *Sergeant* Cifuentes, and the youngest member of the unit, *Private* Ángel Aybar, were given leave to visit their hospitalized comrades. They made a long journey to the rear which would take them to Dno, Riga and Berlin, where they handed out many Iron Crosses. Later *Lieutenant* Otero de Arce would join the group.

JULIAN MARTÍN FABIANI

"Old Guard" Falangist, founder of the SEU (Spanish Students' Union) of the Law Faculty of Madrid's Central University, jailed by the Republicans during the Civil War and one of the fallen of the Battle of Lake Ilmen.

He joined the Blue Division while National Chairman of the SEU and Secretary of the National Delegation Organization Department. At the front he transferred from the 10th Company of the 262nd to the Ski Company. He died during the defence of Maloye Utschno on 19 January 1942.

RAMÓN FARRÉ PALAUS
101% war-disabled

Ramón Farré Palaus was born in Barcelona on 28 March 1920. He spent the Civil War in Barcelona where his brother was murdered by Popular Front sympathizers. He joined the Blue Division and on arrival at the Russian front he served first in the 5th Company of the 263rd before he transferred to the Ski Company. During the lake crossing he suffered from second and third degree frostbite and both his feet were amputated at *Feldlazarett* 510 field hospital. He convalesced in Germany, and in June 1942 in Berlin he was operated on again to tidy up his stumps and fit prostheses. In the summer of 1943 he was back in Spain on leave, but returned to Germany with

a student grant. There, among other activities, he helped recruit Spanish volunteers for the *Waffen SS*.

For his military conduct at Lake Ilmen he was awarded the Iron Cross 2nd Class and he was promoted to infantry corporal, serving in the Invalid Corps. He fell in love with a German woman, with whom he had a daughter, and they set up home in Palma de Mallorca where he worked as a tourist guide. He had already died when, in 1991, his notes on the campaign were published under the title *Impresiones. Centinela junto al Ilmen* (Impressions. Sentry on Lake Ilmen).

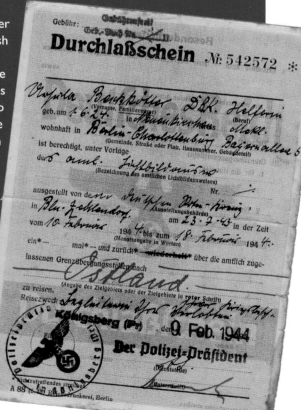

CARLOS SENENT FIGUEROA
Iron Cross, Ilmen survivor

He was born in Madrid on 30 March 1923, the third of five children born to José Senent and Amelia Figueroa who lived on Don Ramón de la Cruz Street. On his father's side his family came from Valencia and Valladolid.

José Senent had a goldsmith's workshop and was a teacher of drawing and art at the *Colegio Caldeiro* school (now the *Colegio Fundación Caldeiro*, of the Amigonian Fathers). In May 1931, on the first night of the burning of convents riot in Madrid, he spent the night at the school with other teachers and parents, prepared to defend the school if it were attacked. Carlos would inherit strong Catholic convictions from his father, as well as extraordinary manual skills.

Carlos's childhood was similar to that of any other child of his age in Spain in the 1930s. Those who knew him said he must have been a young tearaway. His Blue Division friends nicknamed him *Mapamundi* due to all the scars he had, the result of childish pranks gone wrong. Politically he was further to the right than his father; he was a member of *Acción Popular* and in May 1936, when the situation was ready to explode, he joined the *Requeté* of Madrid. He was just 13 years old and had to lie about his age.

When war broke out his father was arrested, jailed in the

1, 2 and 3. Carlos Senent and his fellow soldiers of the Ski Company.

Model Prison of Madrid, and then murdered at Paracuellos in one of the terrible November *sacas,* when political prisoners were taken illegally from prisons and executed. Carlos had to lend his mother a hand; he went around the nearby villages in search of food and earned money by selling wooden models he made of Republican aircraft. On one occasion some militiamen stopped him; they asked to see his documentation and on seeing the surname Figueroa they arrested and held him for a day, believing him to be a member of the aristocracy.

Tragedy also struck the family of the woman who was to be his wife, Paquita Sánchez. Her father, Pedro, a devout Catholic – he belonged to the Nocturnal Adoration – and a member of *Acción Popular*, ran a tyre shop with a partner who helped him out with his deafness problem. Both were arrested by militiamen and summarily executed at the beginning of the war.

In June 1941, having finished high school, Carlos Senent did not hesitate to volunteer *"for the fight against Communism"*. From the letters he sent to his girlfriend during the march to the front we have extracted some lines he wrote. His letters have a touch of humour while reflecting the idealism that helped him endure the rigours of the march, although he always tried to put his reader's mind at rest. On 27 August 1941 he wrote from Poland:

> *"At night we pray the rosary before we go to bed, as getting in touch with God is another great consolation; He is the only one we can call on to help us in our trials and tribulations. We ask Him to keep us safe so that we can return home to embrace our beloved Spain, rewarding us for the pain and suffering we have undergone."*
>
> "On the 4th [of September 1941] they sounded reveille at 3 in the morning, gave out coffee at 3.50 h, and we all left, half asleep, at 4.30 h, with a cold that reminded us of December in Spain. At 10.50 h we passed by a village which, like all those where the reds have been, was burning. At 11.15 h we stopped for lunch. After resting for two hours, on the road again, until 5 in the afternoon when we stopped in a wood for dinner and some sleep after having covered 31 km."

He made a great many friends; one of whom was Eduardo Casanova, who went on to become a TV producer for RTVE. On his way to the front, in October 1941 he formed part of a group of six *divisionarios* who jokingly called themselves *Chuminoskis*; all the members' girlfriends automatically became honorary members.

In November 1941 he transferred from a medical company to the Ski Company, serving in the 1st Platoon. On the banks of Lake Ilmen he got on very well with the civil population. He befriended the son of the Russian family in whose *izba* he was billeted, who he called Sergio. He survived the cold largely due to the fact that the

mamuska in the house he was staying at gave him some Russian felt-lined boots. Thanks to this footwear he avoided frostbite during the lake crossing and survived the operation unscathed.

On returning from Russia he suffered from money problems. Being an ex-Blue Division soldier was of no help in this situation, and he even had to resort to eating at social canteens. His girlfriend's family treated him very well and helped him make ends meet. Gradually his situation began to improve. Carlos worked at the family goldsmith's workshop and drove a taxi, among other jobs. He studied to be a registered nurse and successfully sat the public exams to get a job with the National Welfare Institute, working at the health centre on Avenida Hermanos García Noblejas in Madrid. He retired as administrator of the Dr. Esquerdo health centre.

Carlos married Paquita in 1949 (after nine years of courtship) and had five children: José Pedro, María Carmen, Carlos, Agustín, and María Jesús.

1. Iron Cross 2nd Class awarded to Senent in January 1942. When a small ring on the medal broke, Carlos took advantage of his stay in Riga to have another one made by a specialist jeweller, for which he had to present the citation document.

2. Senent, in the centre, during a patrol on Lake Ilmen.

3. A medal pouch that Carlos Senent carried with him during his time in Russia. It was made from material cut from the shirt that his girlfriend's father (future father-in-law) was wearing when he was murdered by the Popular Front in the Spanish Civil War.

He was a serious but approachable person; an imposing man (not least because of his height) but at the same time charming and affectionate, always willing to help someone in need. He adored his grandchildren, and would take them to the circus or to see the Christmas lights in the centre of Madrid. Carlos was a practising Catholic and a devout follower of the *Virgen del Pilar*.

He was not one to go into details about his time with the Blue Division; it was hard for him to put all he had seen and suffered behind him. Every week he would get together with his fellow *divisionarios* to have a coffee and chat with them. He was a faithful attendee of the annual Blue Division Brotherhood lunch. Although he had excellent friends among the soldiers of the Ski Company, his closest friend dated back to his first posting with the medical company: Celestino García Cordero (Tino), Manuel Font Martínez, and José Guillén Marquina. The latter was an ambulance driver who, with a typically Spanish sense of humour, used to call his ambulance the "*Phänomen*" (Phenomenon in German).

He died of a galloping cancer on 15 September 1995. His wife, Paquita, survived him by nearly twenty years, dying on 31 March 2014.

Senent (second from the right) with a number of *divisionarios* in Madrid, on their return from the campaign. (Senent family collection)

6

Conclusions Regarding Fighting Spirit, Tactics and Strategy

To present-day observers it is perhaps the Ski Company's human and fighting qualities that surprise us most when we read about the operation (crossing the lake and the subsequent battles), the number of casualties suffered, the medals awarded, and the radio dispatches exchanged between *General* Muñoz Grandes and *Captain* Ordás.

We believe that the thumbnail sketches of a number of the protagonists that appear in this book show that the courage, discipline, the spirit of sacrifice and the camaraderie displayed by the unit in battle were based on very firmly held human, military and ideological convictions.

It would seem to be clear that, given the Spanish general's duty to obey a request – nay, order – from his superior officer, from the outset Muñoz Grandes

A Spanish officer, Guillermo Quintana Lacacci, poses in Novgorod in front of a signpost where we can see how close the Blue Division was to Shimsk and Staraya Russa. (Quintana Lacacci family collection)

Ski Company soldier Guillermo González de Canales (second from the left) with another three Spanish volunteers in Riga. Guillermo is holding the teddy bear "Misha". (Guillermo González de Canales)

wanted to showcase both the courage of his men and their willingness to risk their lives to go to the aid of their *Wehrmacht* comrades. It would be fanciful to suggest, as other authors have done, that he acted as he did to deliver a warning that the Spanish would be more than capable of defending their country in the event of an invasion by either Germany or the Allies. But we need to bear in mind that people in general, and those volunteers in particular, do not risk death unless it is for very exalted reasons that should be repeated and refreshed whenever necessary. Muñoz Grandes delivered those stirring words of encouragement to his soldiers simply because they reflected the true spirit with which the Blue Division fought the Russian campaign, and because they were essential to ensure the success of the operation.

At a tactical level, seventy-five years on, the design of the operation continues to arouse interest. How could 200 men be expected to relieve the Vzvad garrison when it was being defended by over twice the number of men and heavy weapons?

In our opinion, once the request for aid was mooted by *General* Chappuis, Blue Division Staff suffered from two information deficits: accurate information concerning the strength of the Vzvad garrison and the extreme Arctic conditions of the lake – the conditions actually prevailing at the time – and an overconfidence in the Ski Company's capabilities of manoeuvre and combat.

Working against the clock and under the pressure of circumstances, *General* Muñoz Grandes and his General Staff, perhaps taken along due to their African War experience – *Colonel* Luis Zanón, Commander of the 3rd Platoon (Operations),

BATTLE OF LAKE ILMEN, JANUARY 1942
OVERALL FIGURES

PARTICIPANTS AND UNINJURED

When we are speaking of a Spanish expeditionary military unit in a combat zone, whose commander had just assumed his duties, it is no easy task to put an accurate figure on the number of men involved in an operation, the number of casualties and medals awarded, or even the men's actual forenames and surnames.

Based on the radio dispatches exchanged between *Captain* Ordás and HQ, most sources put the number of Spaniards who set out from Spasspiskopez and took part in the operation at 206, of which 12 survived unscathed.

We, the authors, have identified 199, among those who set out from Spasspiskopez (195) and the four (three combatants and a radio operator) who caught up with them later. We cannot say with total certainty who those seven other volunteers were – if indeed there really were seven – who also took part in the battle.

With regard to uninjured survivors, it should be noted that sources indicate that there were "Twelve men fit for combat" remaining. However we have identified eighteen. When on 25 January *Captain* Ordás reported the figure as twelve, plus *Sergeant* Foronda of Signals, who certainly could not be considered to be "fit for combat" since he needed to man the radio, it is possible that the other five uninjured survivors were not operationally ready for combat at that precise moment either for some circumstantial reason or because they had been temporarily sent away to perform some task.

CASUALTIES (out of 199)
Killed: 31 (15.5%)
Wounded: 26 (13%)
Frostbite: 123 (61%)

The Individual Military Medal awarded to *Lieutenant* Otero de Arce. (Otero de Arce family collection)

AWARDS (out of 199)
Iron Cross 2nd Class: 35 (17.5%)
Individual Military Medal: 2

One of the 32 Iron Crosses 2nd Class awarded by German High Command as a result of the operation. A further three were awarded later: to Aybar Redondo, Farré Palaus, and Sánchez Bejarano. (Otero de Arce family collection)

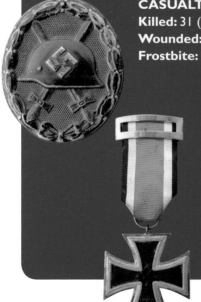

COLLECTIVE MILITARY MEDAL

"Over the frozen waters of Lake Ilmen and thanks to the courage and spirit of sacrifice with which you crossed [the lake] to relieve the heroes of Vsvad, the Spanish lion has roared. On behalf of the Caudillo I award you, Captain Ordás, the Military medal, and to all the courageous troops who were alongside you, the Collective Military Medal. On behalf of our grateful nation I salute you, Muñoz Grandes" (Headquarters of the Blue Division, 27 January 1942).

Major Homar Servera, and Muñoz Grandes's adjutants Cárcer and Lombana, among others, were veterans of the African campaign – thought that the best move was to send a light column like the one that was sent to Vzvad. In the manner of a number of operations carried out in Morocco to aid positions cut off and besieged by the enemy, the Ski Company had the option of hitting its target by surprise, breaking the encirclement, and coming to the aid of the garrison.

The only viable manner for the expedition to advance was on foot. Neither German nor Spanish commanders at any time entertained the fanciful idea of

One of the enemies facing the Spanish. Soviet *Senior Lieutenant* Dmitry Novikov Borisovich fought at Staraya Russa. (Novikov family collection)

transporting the Spanish expeditionaries either by truck or by rail to the Vzvad sector. The XXVIII Army Corps was already moving other forces south of the Ilmen across the ice on foot. "The march will be short" the troops were told at the outset of the operation, because it was expected to be so.

The march was altogether different from what had been expected. The conditions during the lake crossing were beyond extreme. In the weeks after the patrols carried out by the Exploration Group, the brutal drop in temperature had brought about physical changes in the ice, opening up a large number of cracks and pushing up barriers that slowed down the march and forced the column to change course constantly. On the first day of the operation, between the dawns of 10 and 11 January, with no enemy firing on them, over 60 per

A number of convalescing soldiers at Riga in March 1942. On the far right, wearing his Iron Cross earned at Lake Ilmen, Joaquín Escosa San José. The doctor wearing the white coat is *Captain* Pedro Melendo Abad. (Virgilio Hernández Rivadulla)

cent of the Ski Company had been forced to drop out. Never had ice caused so much damage to a Spanish military unit.

We shall never know what might have happened if the Company had not gone off course and had reached Vzvad on 10 January 1942. Having made a shorter journey, frostbite casualties would have been far fewer and the men's fighting capability would have remained practically intact. Around 190 more fighting men in Vzvad would have been a considerable reinforcement. Would they have been able to hold this position for longer, with all that would have meant for German stability south of Lake Ilmen?

Speculation aside, and however much it may undermine Spanish and German propaganda, which from the outset talked up the Blue Division's heroic, emblematic and fraternal act of going to the aid of a German-held position in dire straits, if we look at the Ski Company's performance in the cold harsh light of day we need to face up to some truths. The mission they were entrusted with was not completed, neither at the beginning of the operation nor any time afterwards. The Vzvad garrison broke out of the encirclement using its own resources and when its commanders deemed it necessary.

Once over half of its men had been evacuated after the lake crossing, the Ski Company would take part in a strange battle that would effectively finish it off. As well as the lake crossing, this is the true historical event; the fighting in the sector up until 6 February 1942, the tactical and strategic importance of which has been skimmed over up until now.

1. Joaquín Escosa in the hospital gardens at Riga in April 1942. (Virgilio Hernández Rivadulla)

2. Frostbite victims of the Ski Company, convalescing at Riga in February 1942. From left to right we see Ramón Valentí Abadía (frozen toes), military surgeon Vicente Bádenas Padilla, Carlos Urgoiti y Bas (frozen heel), and Guillermo González de Canales (frozen fingers and toes). (Guillermo González de Canales)

Let us read the words of veteran Ángel Aybar:

> *"They attached us to the Germans and we continued the operation capturing <u>lost villages</u>. As time went by and battles were fought, men died or were evacuated with frostbite. A number of comrades who had been on leave joined us and these reinforcements couldn't have come at a better time. Among them was Martín Fabiani, a friend of mine from Madrid.*
>
> *"He was killed by the Russians shortly after coming under fire for the first time – such a great shame. We were also helped by some Latvian volunteers; with them you felt safe. We understood one another without the need to know each other's language. We were fighting against the same enemy. They were better prepared than us for fighting against the Siberiano skiers."*

The underlining of "lost villages" is ours, because it sums up perfectly the impression the Spaniards had. They were immersed in the fighting with no greater ambition than to survive the cold and the enemy bullets. What possible sense could there be in capturing and recapturing minuscule positions in the middle of those impenetrable forests dotted with snow-covered lowlands? But it did make sense, in fact it made a great deal of sense.

First and foremost it made sense for the German 16th Army. At that time the 16th Army was on the back foot and applying the typically German tactic of

3. Spanish Ski Company soldier with a sub-machine gun. (Via authors)

4. Blue Division men returning from a patrol near Lake Ilmen (Propaganda Company of the 16th Army). (Via authors)

establishing discontinuous lines and hedgehog positions. Every man capable of using a weapon was welcome, so seventy more soldiers was a not inconsiderable reinforcement. But it is clear that the Ski Company's contribution went beyond being an additional grain of sand, beyond any practical effectiveness that those seventy rifles could provide against massive Soviet firepower.

For the German troops on the ground the unexpected arrival of Spanish reinforcements was a major injection of morale, due to the camaraderie they displayed and their special way of fighting. The effect on the enemy was the opposite. Russian prisoners said that they had not been expecting such violent attacks in defence of isolated positions, and less so from Spanish troops. When Morozov's information service discovered that his soldiers, so far to the south of Novgorod, were fighting not only Germans and Latvians but also the Spanish volunteers of the *Galubaya Divisia*, he had the impression – and suffered the real consequences – of there being a German defensive disposition in the sector that was rather more formidable than he had expected.

Those battles in "lost villages" played a very important role. The Spanish, with their German and Latvian comrades, helped establish a discontinuous but effective line of containment to the north of Staraya Russa, which would mitigate the very serious threat to the 16th German Army to the south of Lake Ilmen. The existence of these "lost positions", however small the contingents defending them may have been, constituted a real obstacle to the 11th Army's westward advance. Those few

Present day view of Lake Ilmen, in the heart of winter, with some local fishermen in the distance. The Spanish, unprepared for fighting in Arctic conditions, suffered unspeakable hardships. (AHSR)

Spanish soldiers at Maloye Utschno and the other villages were not only a source of attrition for Morozov's troops, preventing them from advancing on Shimsk, but also collaterally helped keep Staraya Russa in German hands. It is interesting that on the very day the Ski Company survivors reported back at Blue Division HQ on 8 February 1942, two significant events occurred. While at Staraya Russa the encirclement was at last lifted after the road to Cholm was cleared, the Russians closed Demyansk pocket trapping 95,000 German soldiers inside.

At a strategic level, for the Soviet *Stavka* the setback that the Red Army suffered just south of Lake Ilmen frustrated the plans they had made for an offensive on the North-west Front in combination with the Kalinin Front. It was one more setback that contributed to the failure of the great winter counter-offensive masterminded by Stalin across the entire Russian Front. While it achieved some notable partial successes, it fell far short of achieving the ultimate objective which was none other than pushing the Germans back to their June 1941 starting points. Without once letting up in their efforts to capture Staraya Russa, it would be two years before the Russians finally succeeded.

Conversely, for the German OKW, keeping Staraya Russa and its airfield in the hands of the 16th Army eased the situation of Army Group North's south

flank during the first half of 1942. Although Soviet pressure on Staraya Russa and its sector would persist, from that moment on *General* Busch was able to concentrate on feeding and supplying the Demyansk and Cholm pockets, with all that meant in terms of aiding the planning and implementation of German offensive operations on the Russian Front for the summer of 1942.

7

Remembrance and Significance

The Ski Company's commitment and spirit of sacrifice earned the admiration and recognition of the Germans. Based on the number of Iron Crosses awarded, and taking into consideration its size, it was the most decorated unit of all the foreign voluntary forces fighting alongside the *Wehrmacht*.

News of the Spanish action at Lake Ilmen, hailed as a remarkable feat of arms, spread throughout the entire front of Army Group North and the German rearguard. The German propaganda machine ensured that the operation was given the maximum possible coverage on every media, placing emphasis on the alleged liberation of Vzvad.

Three Ski Company men returning to Spain in August 1942, with the satisfaction of having done their duty. On the right, "*El Maño*", Guillermo González de Canales, and Ramón Valentí. (Guillermo González de Canales)

A cartoon by José María Nieto, a cartoonist from Valladolid, making a satirical comment on the illogicality and sectarianism currently prevailing in Spain regarding the public recognition of historical characters and episodes. The "Historical Memory Act" passed in 2007 effectively demonizes anything to do with Franco and the winning side in the Civil War, including the Blue Division. The cartoonist chose the Lake Ilmen exploit and the attempts to change the name of the street that honours the Blue Division dead as the vehicle for his cartoon (José María Nieto, ABC, 3 January 2016).

The OKW was fully aware of what was happening in the sector – it was Hitler who gave the order for Vzvad to be abandoned and for a withdrawal to a more easily held position –, another reason why the Führer himself should mention publicly, at the *Reichstag*, the help provided by the Blue Division south of Lake Ilmen.

In the imagination of Germans and Spaniards alike, especially among those who fought in Army Group North and their descendants, this episode would last until the present day. It symbolizes, in the most

Front cover of the war diary of José Guillén Marquina, an honorary member of the Ski Company. His family still keeps his unpublished book entitled: *A year [fighting] against the Bolshevik hordes*. (Family collection)

CONGRATULATORY DISPATCHES FROM GERMAN COMMANDERS

Ernst Busch, commander of the 16th Army North, to Muñoz Grandes:

"General: On your birthday [27 January] I'd like to express my sincerest congratulations and wish you future triumphs at the head of your superb division in our common cause. I'd like to take this opportunity to also express my special appreciation of the courageous members of your division who, in order to relieve the position at Vsvad, advanced over Lake Ilmen and then, united in a loyal spirit of camaraderie with the troops of the 81st Division, performed such exceptional feats, both in defence and in attack. This undertaking, one of true camaraderie, receives the utmost praise from the entire army and is cause for you and all the men in your Division to be immensely satisfied. I wish you, my General, and your brave Division, the very best of luck and many more triumphs. I remain respectfully yours. Von Busch."

Erich H. Schopper, commander of the 81st Infantry Division, to Muñoz Grandes:

"My most respected General: Now, when the courageous soldiers of your Ski Company are no longer under my command, it is my inescapable duty to express my gratitude to you and my admiration for the fearless and heroic bravery of your soldiers. It was an honour for me to have these excellent troops under my command. The thirty-two Iron Crosses awarded to the [Ski] Company as a tangible expression of High Command's recognition [of their bravery] also gives me special satisfaction. In the hope that I can congratulate you in person and convey my esteem, I remain respectfully yours, Schopper."

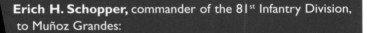

expressive manner possible, the meaning and the essence of the Blue Division's campaign on the Russian Front.

We would like to close this book by remembering each and every soldier who took part in the battle to the south of Lake Ilmen: Spaniards, Germans, Latvians, and Russians. Brought together under different circumstances, they wrote a history of blood and hardship, in many cases tinged with heroism. Some died and others were wounded or frostbitten, often with life-changing consequences. What they experienced allows the Europeans of today to resolve our differences peacefully and conserve the most noble and diverse elements of our millenary culture.

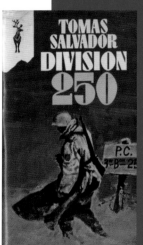

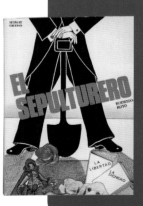

THE HEROIC ACTION AT LAKE ILMEN IN LITERATURE

The Ski Company's action was widely disseminated by the press, and also by word of mouth at the front and by the *divisionarios* when they arrived back in Spain. Almost immediately the Spanish exploit also began to be the subject of literary works.

Of the abundant Blue Division bibliography we would highlight the writers and *divisionarios* Fernando Vadillo and Tomás Salvador, both eminent historians of the great unit. *Arrabales de Leningrad* (Outskirts of Leningrad) and *División 250* covered the Lake Ilmen action in several chapters. Based on their respective wartime experiences and the testimonies of some of its protagonists, they succeed in capturing the chaotic harshness of the crossing and of the fighting that took place to the south of the lake. Other authors and historians have also dealt with this historic event, in more or less depth and with more or less historical rigour. This is the case of Rodrigo Royo, also a *divisionario*, who in 1975 published the Planeta award finalist novel *El sepulturero* (The Gravedigger), the protagonist of which, Julián Rovira, is a Lake Ilmen veteran who remains faithful to his Falangist principles.

In 1942, with the Blue Division still at the Russian Front, two simple works were published: *Fraternidad en el campo de batalla* and *Un episodio de la Compañía de Esquiadores en el lago Ilmen* (Fraternity on the Battlefield and An episode of the Ski Company at Lake Ilmen). *Fraternidad* (published by the *Academia de Infantería*) consists of transcriptions of the radio messages exchanged between *Captain* Ordás and Blue Division command, while the second short book (published by Dédalo) includes not only an article on Lake Ilmen by the journalist Manuel Aznar, but mentions one of the heroes of Lake Ilmen, Carlos Urgoiti y Bas.

The latter, Urgoiti y Bas, was the first Ski Company veteran to turn his hand to writing on the subject of the Ilmen epic. In 1987 he wrote a short text, *Prólogo al tema amistad* (Prologue to the matter of friendship), highlighting the bonds of camaraderie and fraternity that arose among those who took part in the operation. Without a doubt, an original and human approach to what was the terrible experience of those days of January 1942. The work of another survivor, Ramón Farré Palaus, entitled *Impresiones: Centinela junto al Ilmen* (Impressions: Sentry on Lake Ilmen) was published a little later. This is doubly interesting because the prologue was written by another Ski Company veteran, Guillermo Ruiz Gijón.

In 1994, Eduardo Barrachina Juan, a Catalonian magistrate and prolific writer, published *La batalla del Lago Ilmen* (The Battle of Lake Ilmen), an essential work of great historical worth, in which he makes an in-depth analysis of what happened during and after the lake crossing.

The liberation of the Vzvad garrison by the Spanish also had a certain repercussion on German post-war military literature. In the collection *Soldatengeschichten aus äller Welt (Soldiers' tales from around the world)*, Russian campaign experts Werner Haupt and Fred Nemis each devote an issue to this topic: number 99, *Die blaue Division*, and number 174, *Todesmarsch über den Ilmensee* (Death march over Lake Ilmen). It should be noted that Haupt (1923-2005) served as a *Second Lieutenant* in the Anti-Tank Group of the 81st Infantry Division and had first-hand knowledge of the events of Lake Ilmen. His work was republished in Germany in the 1990s in the *Der Landser* collection, with the eloquent title *Die Eishölle am Ilmensee* (Lake Ilmen Ice Hell), and was published twice more in Spanish: once in 1962, published by Marte, entitled *La División Azul junto al lago Ilmen* (The Blue Division on the banks of Lake Ilmen) and a second time in 2016, published by Titania, entitled *La División Azul, la epopeya del lago Ilmen* (The Blue Division, the epic feat of Lake Ilmen).

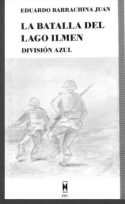

Appendix

Spanish Participants in the Crossing and Battle of Lake Ilmen, 10 January–8 February 1942

The following list has been compiled by the authors, using as a basis the list provided by Eduardo Barrachina in his book (see Bibliography), which we corroborated to the extent that we were able. It is, of course, not definitive and we would be grateful to any readers for any correction of or addition to the list.

MEN BELONGING TO THE SKI COMPANY				
SURNAMES & FORENAME	RANK	UNIT	OUTCOME	IRON CROSS 2nd CLASS (EK 2)
Otero de Arce, José	Lieut.	Staff	Frostbite	+
Polanco y Drake, Leandro	Sergeant	Staff	Frostbite	+
Alonso Hernández, Ángel	Corporal	Staff	Survived uninjured	+
Salas, Juan	Corporal	Staff	Frostbite	
Delgado, Ricardo	Corporal	Staff	Frostbite	
Moya, Antonio	Private	Staff	Killed (missing)	
Amat, Teodoro	Private	Staff	Frostbite	
Barbasán Larrea, Mariano	Private	Staff	Killed (missing)	
Herrero Granados, Manuel	Private	Staff	Wounded	+
Marcos Rivero, Ángel	Private	Staff	Survived uninjured	+
Aybar Redondo, Ángel	Private	Staff	Survived uninjured	+
Martín Cuellar, José	Private	Staff	Frostbite	
Bergé, León	Private	Staff	Wounded	+
Mediavilla Fuentes, Juan José	Private	Staff	Frostbite	
Amoz Aguirre, León	Private	Staff	Frostbite	+
Mont Serrano, Álvaro	Private	Staff	Frostbite	
Martín Fabiani, Julián*	Private	Staff	Killed	
Castañer Ensenat, Vicente	Lieut.	1st Platoon	Survived uninjured	
Montaña Orduña, Cayetano	Sergeant	1st Platoon	Killed	
Díez López, Manuel	Corporal	1st Platoon	Frostbite	
García Berenguer, Agustín	Corporal	1st Platoon	Killed	
Muñoz Simón, Manuel	Corporal	1st Platoon	Killed	
Hernández Bravo, Jorge*	Corporal	1st Platoon	Frostbite	
Ruiz Gijón, Guillermo	Private	1st Platoon	Wounded	+

MEN BELONGING TO THE SKI COMPANY				
SURNAMES & FORENAME	RANK	UNIT	OUTCOME	IRON CROSS 2nd CLASS (EK 2)
Urgoiti y Bas, Carlos	Private	1st Platoon	Frostbite	
Senent Figueroa, Carlos	Private	1st Platoon	Survived uninjured	+
Farré Palaus, Ramón	Private	1st Platoon	Wounded	+
Valero Martín, Napoleón	Private	1st Platoon	Frostbite	
Valentí Abadía, Ramón	Private	1st Platoon	Frostbite	
González de Canales, Guillermo	Private	1st Platoon	Frostbite	
Vélez García, José Luis	Private	1st Platoon	Frostbite	
Coscolla Teixidor, Alberto	Private	1st Platoon	Frostbite	
Muriel Fernández, Félix	Private	1st Platoon	Frostbite	
Hernández Rivadulla, Virgilio*	Private	1st Platoon	Frostbite	+
Sánchez-Covisa Carro, Mariano	Private	1st Platoon	Frostbite	+
García García, Marcos	Private	1st Platoon	Frostbite	
Escosa San José, Osvaldo Joaquín	Private	1st Platoon	Wounded	+
Monrach, Andrés	Private	1st Platoon	Frostbite	
Piernavieja del Pozo, Miguel	Private	1st Platoon	Wounded	+
García Porta, Antonio	Lieut.	2nd Platoon	Wounded	+
Ferrer Andrés, Rafael	Sergeant	2nd Platoon	Survived uninjured	+
Díaz Garay, Rufino	Sergeant	2nd Platoon	Killed	
Monteagudo Monteagudo, Manuel	Corporal	2nd Platoon	Frostbite	
Salmerón, Juan Manuel	Corporal	2nd Platoon	Frostbite	
Malvat, José	Corporal	2nd Platoon	Killed (missing)	
Gómez Martínez, Emilio	Corporal	2nd Platoon	Frostbite	
Berenguer Benito, José	Private	2nd Platoon	Frostbite	
Taboada, José Luis	Private	2nd Platoon	Frostbite	
Vázquez Roy, Germán	Private	2nd Platoon	Killed (missing)	
Moreno Filló, José Luis	Private	2nd Platoon	Frostbite	
García Armengol, Pedro	Private	2nd Platoon	Killed	
Bocos de la Fuente, Francisco	Private	2nd Platoon	Frostbite	
Archely Fernández, Tomás	Private	2nd Platoon	Wounded	
Moll Pérez, Ismael	Private	2nd Platoon	Frostbite	
Rodríguez Alba, Manuel	Private	2nd Platoon	Frostbite	
Cuteros López, Pedro	Private	2nd Platoon	Frostbite	
Mur Cajal, Ramón	Private	2nd Platoon	Frostbite	
Vera Encarnación, José	Private	2nd Platoon	Wounded	
Ayuso Mañu, Antonio	Private	2nd Platoon	Frostbite	
Mera Valiente, Valentín	Private	2nd Platoon	Frostbite	
Colmán Notoro, Crisanto	Private	2nd Platoon	Frostbite	
Bagés, José	Private	2nd Platoon	Wounded	

MEN BELONGING TO THE SKI COMPANY				
SURNAMES & FORENAME	RANK	UNIT	OUTCOME	IRON CROSS 2nd CLASS (EK 2)
Bellver Soler, José	Private	2nd Platoon	Killed	
Manso de Castro, Juan	Private	2nd Platoon	Frostbite	
Velasco del Val, Jacinto	Lieut.	3rd Platoon	Wounded	
Sánchez López, Juan Antonio	Sergeant	3rd Platoon	Wounded	
Sánchez Gutiérrez, Patrocinio	Sergeant	3rd Platoon	Frostbite	
Jiménez, José	Corporal	3rd Platoon	Frostbite	
De la Cuesta, Carlos	Corporal	3rd Platoon	Frostbite	
Hortiguela Fernández, Antolín	Corporal	3rd Platoon	Wounded	
Andrés, Simón	Private	3rd Platoon	Wounded	
Gil Sánchez, Mateo	Private	3rd Platoon	Frostbite	
Galán, Enrique	Private	3rd Platoon	Wounded	
Medina, Miguel	Private	3rd Platoon	Wounded	
Giménez Huerta, José	Private	3rd Platoon	Frostbite	
Bas Martínez, Fernando	Private	3rd Platoon	Frostbite	
Pozos, José María	Private	3rd Platoon	Frostbite	
Crispí Babiloni, José	Private	3rd Platoon	Frostbite	
Castillo, José	Private	3rd Platoon	Frostbite	
Meijido, Antonio	Private	3rd Platoon	Frostbite	
Comas Palau, José	Private	3rd Platoon	Frostbite	
Oliva Pérez, Nicanor	Private	3rd Platoon	Frostbite	
Talón Canut, Fernando	Private	3rd Platoon	Frostbite	
Bernabéu del Amo, Germán	2nd Lieut.	4th Platoon	Frostbite	
Granada Aspa, José Antonio	Sergeant	4th Platoon	Frostbite	
Bernardo Rodrigo, Antonio	Sergeant	4th Platoon	Frostbite	
Cáceres Ruiz, Ernesto	Corporal	4th Platoon	Frostbite	
Rivero, Enrique	Corporal	4th Platoon	Frostbite	
Martín Enciso, Joaquín	Corporal	4th Platoon	Frostbite	
Manzano San Higinio, Pascual	Corporal	4th Platoon	Wounded	
Giménez Suárez, Nicolás	Corporal	4th Platoon	Wounded	
Sánchez Villanueva, Teodosio	Private	4th Platoon	Killed	
Pascual Santos, Avelino	Private	4th Platoon	Killed	
Vergara Morales, Antonio	Private	4th Platoon	Frostbite	
Ramoy, Antonio	Private	4th Platoon	Survived uninjured	
Ruiz Cabadas, Plácido	Private	4th Platoon	Frostbite	
Merino Callejo, José	Private	4th Platoon	Frostbite	
Navarro Santamarta, Julio	Private	4th Platoon	Frostbite	
Otermín Altamira, Luis	Private	4th Platoon	Frostbite	
Rodríguez García, Natalio	Private	4th Platoon	Wounded	

MEN BELONGING TO THE SKI COMPANY				
SURNAMES & FORENAME	RANK	UNIT	OUTCOME	IRON CROSS 2nd CLASS (EK 2)
Gutiérrez Polanco, Jesús	Private	4th Platoon	Wounded	
Álvarez Fernández, Manuel	Private	4th Platoon	Frostbite	
Suárez Martínez, Rafael	Private	4th Platoon	Wounded	
Gutiérrez Royón, Jerónimo	Private	4th Platoon	Frostbite	
García Alonso, José	Private	4th Platoon	Frostbite	
Medina González, Miguel	Private	4th Platoon	Frostbite	
Pérez Losantos, Ricardo	Private	4th Platoon	Frostbite	
Giménez Moreno, Francisco	Private	4th Platoon	Frostbite	
Gordón Gordón, Luis	Private	4th Platoon	Frostbite	
Martínez, Manuel	Private	4th Platoon	Frostbite	
Martínez Acevedo, José	Private	4th Platoon	Frostbite	
García Larios, Joaquín	2nd Lieut.	5th Platoon	Killed (missing)	
Schumacher Auslander, Miguel	Sergeant	5th Platoon	Killed	
Mortes Martínez, Joaquín	Sergeant	5th Platoon	Frostbite	
García del Valle Gámez, Francisco	Corporal	5th Platoon	Killed (d. Slotzy Hospital)+	
Mariño Barrios, Julio	Corporal	5th Platoon	Killed	
García Rey, Eugenio	Corporal	5th Platoon	Frostbite	
Cañedo Aguilar, Feliciano	Corporal	5th Platoon	Killed	
Díaz González, Ignacio	Private	5th Platoon	Frostbite	
Goy Benítez, Pedro	Private	5th Platoon	Frostbite	
Vela, Ángel	Private	5th Platoon	Killed	
Rivas, José	Private	5th Platoon	Frostbite	
Sanchís Sánchez, Manuel	Private	5th Platoon	Killed	
Cucala Bastida, Gustavo	Private	5th Platoon	Frostbite	
Vidal, Antonio	Private	5th Platoon	Frostbite	
Ceballos Llaca, José (María)	Private	5th Platoon	Killed	
Martínez Laredo, Fernando	Private	5th Platoon	Killed	
Jiménez Cámara, Manuel	Private	5th Platoon	Wounded	
Martínez Bonaechea, José	Private	5th Platoon	Frostbite	
López de Castro, Manuel	Private	5th Platoon	Frostbite	
Garrigós, Julio	Private	5th Platoon	Frostbite	
Muñoz Cassani, Juan	Private	5th Platoon	Killed	
Blázquez Rodríguez, Ángel	Private	5th Platoon	Killed	
López de Santiago, Alfonso	2nd Lieut.	6th Platoon	Wounded	+
Maíllo Llamas, Primo	Sergeant	6th Platoon	Frostbite	
Sánchez Escudero, José	Sergeant	6th Platoon	Killed	
Bautista Molina, Ricardo	Corporal	6th Platoon	Survived uninjured	
Martín Gallego, José	Corporal	6th Platoon	Killed (missing)	

MEN BELONGING TO THE SKI COMPANY				
SURNAMES & FORENAME	RANK	UNIT	OUTCOME	IRON CROSS 2nd CLASS (EK 2)
Pagador, Solidario	Corporal	6th Platoon	Frostbite	
Martínez Cantizano, Juan	Corporal	6th Platoon	Frostbite	
Segura, Manuel	Private	6th Platoon	Killed	
Carriazo Calvo, Francisco	Private	6th Platoon	Frostbite	
Pérez Lezama, Jesús	Private	6th Platoon	Frostbite	
Valdés Baró, Emilio	Private	6th Platoon	Killed	
Pinés Fernández, Ángel	Private	6th Platoon	Frostbite	
Tejeiro Oliveira, Francisco	Private	6th Platoon	Frostbite	
Sotomayor, Manuel	Private	6th Platoon	Frostbite	
González Collado, Vicente	Private	6th Platoon	Frostbite	
Valentín Valentín, José	Private	6th Platoon	Killed	
Santiago Medina, Francisco	Private	6th Platoon	Frostbite	
César Fernández, Manuel	Private	6th Platoon	Frostbite	
Jiménez Nieto, Agustín	Private	6th Platoon	Frostbite	
Gonzalvo González, Ángel	Private	6th Platoon	Killed	
Barrio, Alberto	Private	6th Platoon	Frostbite	
Ferrera, Antonio	Private		6th Platoon	Survived uninjured
Martín Martín, José	Private	6th Platoon	Killed	
Pedraza, Francisco	Private	6th Platoon	Frostbite	
Jiménez Nieto, Francisco	Private	6th Platoon	Survived uninjured	

(*) Did not cross Lake Ilmen; joined the battle later.

MEN ATTACHED FROM OTHER UNITS				
Ordás Rodríguez, José Manuel	Captain	3rd Anti-Tank Coy	Survived uninjured	+
Cifuentes Langa, Santiago	Sergeant (med)	3rd Anti-Tank Coy	Survived uninjured	+
Otero Carballo, Román	Sergeant	3rd Anti-Tank Coy	Frostbite	+
Rodríguez Patón, Luis	Corporal	3rd Anti-Tank Coy	Frostbite	+
Navarro, Aurelio	Corporal	3rd Anti-Tank Coy	Frostbite	
Santos Conejo, Ángel	Private	3rd Anti-Tank Coy	Wounded	+
Fraga Rodríguez, Luis	Private	3rd Anti-Tank Coy	Frostbite	+
De la Vega Gómez, José	Private	3rd Anti-Tank Coy	Survived uninjured	+
Del Riego, Guillermo	Private	3rd Anti-Tank Coy	Wounded	+
Muñoz, José	Private	3rd Anti-Tank Coy	Frostbite	
Domínguez Díaz, Bernardino	Lieutenant	Exploration Gr.	Survived uninjured	+
Sánchez Bejarano, Pedro	Lieut. (med)	Exploration Gr.	Survived uninjured	+

MEN ATTACHED FROM OTHER UNITS				
Goguidjonachvili, Konstantino	Lieut. (interpr)	Exploration Gr.	Frostbite	
Fernández Molina, José Antonio	Sergeant	Exploration Gr.	Survived uninjured	+
Galán, Sebastián	Private	Exploration Gr.	Survived uninjured	+
Cabre Bihliugmaier, Federico	Private	Exploration Gr.	Frostbite	+
Rodríguez Martínez, José	Private	Exploration Gr.	Frostbite	
Pérez Pérez, Cristóbal	Corporal	Reserve Batt.	Frostbite	
Lequerica Líbano, Domingo	Private	Reserve Batt.	Frostbite	
Martínez Martínez, Eduardo	Private	Reserve Batt.	Frostbite	
García Tamayo, José	Private	Reserve Batt.	Frostbite	
Suárez Álvarez, José María	Private	Reserve Batt.	Frostbite	
Sanz Gurri, José	Private	Reserve Batt.	Frostbite	
García Núñez, Manuel	Private	Reserve Batt.	Frostbite	
Soteras Cuenca, Marcelino	Private	Reserve Batt.	Frostbite	
Ruiz Martínez, Pablo	Private	Reserve Batt.	Frostbite	
Rodríguez Prat, Rafael	Private	Reserve Batt.	Frostbite	
Madero Fernández, José	Private	Reserve Batt.	Frostbite	
Novo Cadierno, Benigno	Private	Reserve Batt.	Frostbite	
Moreno Núñez, Manuel	Private	Veterinary Gr.	Frostbite	
Márquez Jarillo, Manuel	Private	Veterinary Gr.	Frostbite	
Mateo Durán, Manuel	Private	Veterinary Gr.	Frostbite	
Gallardo, Luis	Private	Veterinary Gr.	Frostbite	
González, Elías	Private	Veterinary Gr.	Frostbite	
Sanz Marchena, Manuel	Private	Veterinary Gr.	Frostbite	
Fernández, Antonio	Private	Veterinary Gr.	Frostbite	
García Ontiveros, Francisco	Sergeant	Radio Coy - Signals Gr.	Wounded	+
Foronda Zudaire, Rafael	Sergeant	Radio Coy - Signals Gr.	Survived uninjured	+
Díaz Garcés, Martín	Corporal	Radio Coy - Signals Gr.	Frostbite	
Garrido Jiménez/Herrero, Francisco	Private	Radio Coy - Signals Gr.	Frostbite	+
Casado Martín, Manuel *	Private	Radio Coy - Signals Gr.		

(*) Joined the operation in its final stages.

Sources

1. DOCUMENTARY SOURCES. ARCHIVES CONSULTED:
   - **General Military Archive (Avila)**
     Collection of the Spanish Division of Volunteers/General Staff/General Operational Orders/Divisional Orders/Information Bulletins
   - **General Military Archive (Segovia)**
     Collection of the Army Ministry/Personnel
   - **Historical Memory Documentation Centre (Salamanca)**
     Dionisio Ridruejo Collection
   - **Private archives (various locations)**
     César Ibáñez Cagna, family of Ángel Alonso Hernández, family of the brothers Tomás and Jesús Archely Fernández, Ángel Aybar Redondo, family of Alberto Coscolla Teixidor, Carlos Caballero Jurado, family of Francisco García Ontiveros, Guillermo González de Canales López, family of José Guillén Marquina, Virgilio Hernández Rivadulla, Manuel Liñán, Juan Negreira, family of José Manuel Ordás Rodríguez, family of José Otero de Arce, family of Senent Figueroa, and family of Jesús Zaera León.

2. TESTIMONIES OF EX-COMBATANTS AND RELATIVES OF EX-COMBATANTS OF THE SKI COMPANY (FIRST CONTINGENT):
   - Family of Ángel Alonso Hernández, Corporal, Ski Company.
   - Family of the brothers Tomás and Jesús Archely Fernández. Both privates, the former was a combatant in the Anti-Tank Group and Ski Company.
   - Ángel Aybar Redondo. Private, Radio Company of the Signals Group and Ski Company.
   - Family of Alberto Coscolla Teixidor. Private, Staff Battery of the 1st Group of the 250th Artillery Regiment and Ski Company.
   - Family of Francisco García Ontiveros. Sergeant, Radio Company of the Signals Group and attached to the Ski Company.
   - O.S. (he wished to remain anonymous). Private, Gunner and Ski Company.
   - Guillermo González de Canales López. Private, Veterinary Company, Animal Butchery Company (Quartermaster Group) and Ski Company.
   - Virgilio Hernández Rivadulla. Private, 1st Ambulance Platoon of the Medical Group and Ski Company.
   - Family of Álvaro Mont Serrano. Private, Signals Group and Ski Company.
   - Family of José Manuel Ordás Rodríguez. Captain, 3rd Anti-Tank Company attached to the Ski Company.
   - Family of José Otero de Arce. Lieutenant, 7th Artillery Battery, Ski Company, Field Gendarmerie and Representation of the Blue Division in Berlin.

- Family of Guillermo Ruiz Gijón, Private, 10th Company of the 262nd Regiment and Ski Company.
- Family of Carlos Senent Figueroa, Private, 1st Company of the Medical Group and Ski Company.

3. OTHER TESTIMONIES OF INTEREST:
- Family of José (Pepe) Guillén Marquina. Private of the 1st Platoon and 2nd Motorized Ambulance Platoon of the Medical Group. He wanted to join the Ski Company in November 1941 but was unable to as he was stationed at Otenski. For the ex-combatants group of the unit based in Madrid, with whom he had strong ties, he was considered to be an honorary member of the Division.
- Family of José María Gutiérrez del Castillo. General Secretary of the SEU, Blue Division volunteer, 1st Motorized Ambulance Platoon, leader and friend of the members of the SEU in the Ski Company.
- María Cristina Orive Alonso. Falangist nurse in the Blue Division and wife of Agustín Payno Mendicouague, medic with the 1st Anti-Tank Company, deployed in the Lake Ilmen sector.
- Family of Jesús Zaera León. Volunteer private in the 3rd Anti-Tank Company, a unit that fought alongside the Ski Company.

4. BIBLIOGRAPHY, ARTICLES, DIARIES AND NEWSPAPERS:

BOOKS:
- AZNAR, MANUEL, *Un episodio de la Compañía de Esquiadores en el Lago Ilmen*, Dédalo, Madrid 1942.
- BARRACHINA JUAN, EDUARDO, *La Batalla del Lago Ilmen*, PPU, Barcelona 1994.
- CABALLERO JURADO, CARLOS, *División Azul: Estructura de una Fuerza de Combate*, Galland Books, Valladolid 2011.
  Españoles contra Stalin: La División Azul en el frente del Voljov. Octubre de 1941-agosto de 1942, Susaeta, Madrid 2016.
- FORCZYK, ROBERT, *Demyansk 1942-1942: The frozen fortress*, Osprey, Oxford 2012.
- HAUPT, WERNER, *Die blaue Division: Die spanische Freiwilligen-Division kämpft eingeschlossenen deutschen Stützpunkt am Ilmensee frei*, Arthur Moewig, Munich 1959.
  La División Azul junto al lago Ilmen, Marte, Barcelona 1962.
- HOFFMANN, KARL-OTTO, *Ln–Die Geschichte der Luftnachrichtentruppe Band II – Der Weltkrieg. Teil 1: Der Flugmelde- und Jägerleitdienst 1939-1945*, Kurt Vowinckel Verlag, Neckargemünd 1968.
- NEMIS, FRED, *Todesmarsch über den Ilmensee*, Arthur Moewig, Munich 1958.
- PINILLA, ÁNGEL G, *Héroes entre valientes*, Ágora, Madrid 2012.

– SALVADOR ESPESO, TOMÁS, *División 250*, Destino, Barcelona 1962.
– VADILLO ORTIZ DE GUZMÁN, FERNANDO, *Arrabales de Leningrado I*, García Hispán, Alicante 1992.

ARTICLES:
– GARCÍA-BERNARDO, JORGE ÁLVAREZ, *El entorno estratégico de las operaciones ofensivas y defensivas de la División Azul, 1941-1943*, Aportes. Revista de Historia Contemporánea no. 61, ACTAS, Madrid 2006.
– IBÁÑEZ CAGNA, CÉSAR, *El invierno de 1941-42, en Rusia*, Extra Defensa no. 16, Madrid June 1991.
– MARÍN FERRER, EMILIO, *Valientes en el Ilmen. Esquiadores españoles en Rusia*, Fuerza Terrestre no. 48, Madrid 2008.
– SUÁREZ-DAPEYRE, NARCISO, *El Ilmen y el Ladoga. Heroísmo español en Rusia*, Extra Defensa no. 53, Madrid May 1999.
– TORRES GARCÍA, FRANCISCO, *Los españoles entran en la Leyenda*, Documentos Fuerza Nueva no. 24, Madrid 1991.

DIARIES AND MEMOIRS
– COSCOLLA TEIXIDOR, ALBERTO, Memoirs entitled *33 Cruces de Hierro sobre el Ilmen* (published in the *Blau División* [sic] *Newsletter* of the Hermandad Provincial de Alicante).
– FARRÉ PALAUS, RAMÓN, *Impresiones. Centinela junto al Ilmen*, editorial García Hispán, Alicante 1991.
– GONZÁLEZ DE CANALES LÓPEZ, GUILLERMO, Russian campaign diary, notations, sketches and war poetry (Family collection).
– GUILLÉN MARQUINA, JOSÉ, Diary (Family collection).
– GUTIÉRREZ DEL CASTILLO, JOSÉ MARÍA, Diary of his time in the Blue Division and several personal notations (published in the *Blau División Newsletter*).
– URGOITI Y BAS, CARLOS, *Coloquios en Larra. Prólogo al tema Amistad*, Dédalo, Madrid 1987.
– ZAERA LEÓN, JESÚS, Diary of his time in the Blue Division (published in the *Blau División Newsletter*) and letters from the front (Family collection).

5. MAIN INTERNET RESOURCES:
bibliotecavirtualdefensa.es
facebook.com (Homenaje nacional a la División Azul)
hemeroteca.abc.es
hemeroteca.LaVanguard.com
memoriablau.foros
prensahistorica.mcu.es
wikipedia.es